Fred E. Sistler

The farm computer

Reston Publishing Co., Inc.
A Prentice-Hall Company
Reston, Virginia

Library of Congress Cataloging in Publication Data

Sistler, Fred E.
  The farm computer.

  Includes index.
    1. Farm management—Data processing.   2. Agriculture—
Data processing.   3. Microcomputers.   I. Title.
S565.7.S57   1984   630′.2′0854   83-13937
ISBN 0-8359-1862-9 (c)
ISBN 0-8359-1861-0 (paper)

© 1984 by Reston Publishing Co., Inc.
A Prentice-Hall Company
Reston, Virginia 22090

10 9 8 7 6 5 4 3 2 1

Printed in the United States of America

To the people in agribusiness, with the hope that the material in this book will help them to provide food for a hungry world; and to my wife, Audrey, and my son, David, who gave up so much for me to write it.

Contents

Chapter 6 • Machinery management, 100

Chapter 7 • Livestock production, 128

Chapter 8 • Crop production, 138

Chapter 9 • Chemical application, 152

Chapter 10 • Greenhouses and nurseries, 164

Preface

A small sign on top of a computer read, "This machine could do the work of 20 people if we could just find one person who knew how to make it work." Another sign read, "This machine is the ultimate in technology. A sense of awe is in order." These are too often the feelings that people have about computers. A computer is some kind of strange machine with lights and buttons and controls that can do all kinds of marvelous things from playing games with children to cooking a meal, to keeping financial records, to guiding man and machine through the heavens. They seem to be so smart that an ordinary person cannot even talk with them or understand them.

Until recently, most of us did not have to concern ourselves with computers because we never saw them. The closest we came to them was when we received some bill on a card with holes in it that had a warning about not bending, folding, or mutilating. If there was ever a problem with the bill, it was because the computer must have made a mistake. Once computer billing began, it seemed as if people quit making mistakes, and the computers made all of them. Occasionally, we saw some big computer in a flight control center on television when a rocket was being launched. In college not too many years ago, some of us carried a deck of computer cards to a window where they were somehow "fed" into a computer that we never touched or were even allowed to see.

But things are changing rapidly. Small computers (called microcomputers) are popping up everywhere. They are in our microwave ovens, dishwashers, clothes dryers, electric drills; in video games that plug into our televisions; and in the televisions themselves. There are little computers for our families with friendly names like PET and APPLE and PINEAPPLE.

As these small, personal computer systems (Apple, Atari, PET, Radio Shack, etc.) become more affordable to the general public, questions arise like "How good are these things?," "If they are good, what are they good for?," "What can I reasonably expect a computer to do for me, and how much do I have to know to get it to work?," and "I have a job to do and I need a computer to do it—what kind do I need?"

This book is written to help people in agriculturally related fields answer some of these questions. It assumes that you are not familiar with the technical language of computers. It also assumes that you are more interested in learning how to use a computer to solve problems than in understanding the details of what is happening inside the machine. What occurs within the machine will not be discussed except when understanding details is necessary to perform a given task. This book deals with microcomputing systems that are available for a few thousand dollars or less.

This book is written to help you understand that personal computers can do many useful things for you; that they do not have to be intimidating; and that while they cannot do your thinking for you, they can make your work, time, and decision-making abilities more productive. Sample programs are included in the book as a basis for you to develop your own programs. All of the programs listed in this book have been tested on a Radio Shack Model II microcomputer.

You will probably find that computers have a lot in common with people. They are not always easy to understand and none of them will do everything you want them to do. But the more you learn about them, the more you grow to like them and appreciate them for what they are and how they can do so many good and useful things.

The farm computer

Chapter 1
Introduction to computers

A computer is an electronic machine that performs a series of explicit instructions. These instructions may be something as simple as adding two numbers or as complex as simulating the nuclear reactions occurring within our sun. A computer can collect information, manipulate it, store it, display the information in various forms (words, graphs, pictures, etc.), create new information, monitor events, and control objects and processes. Some can even listen and talk.

There are three broad categories of computers, although recent advances in integrated circuit technology are making these groups less distinguishable. The three categories are mainframe computers, mini-computers, and microcomputers.

The Mainframe Computer

Mainframe computers are the large machines that people think of when they envision a huge room full of equipment with flashing lights, reels of spinning magnetic tapes, and people walking around in white lab coats. (See Figures 1-1 through 1-3.) These computers are usually kept in an environment where the temperature and humidity are closely controlled.

Mainframe computers have a large amount of memory for holding programs and data (often several million pieces of information at one time). They have several storage devices for programs and data, including both hard disk drives and large magnetic tape units, high-speed printers, punched card readers, and card punches. (See Figures 1-4 and 1-5.) They can support several computer terminals simultaneously at many remote locations. Mainframe computers can execute hundreds of thousands of operations per second. They are powerful, very fast, and expensive—

Figure 1-1 • IBM® 3033 Multiprocessor Complex (courtesy of the International Business Machines Corporation)

Figure 1-2 • IBM® 4341 Processor (courtesy of the International Business Machines Corporation)

Figure 1-3 • Radio Shack® Color™ Computer (courtesy of Radio Shack®, a division of the Tandy Corporation)

Figure 1-4 • IBM® 3262 Line Printer (courtesy of the International Business Machines Corporation)

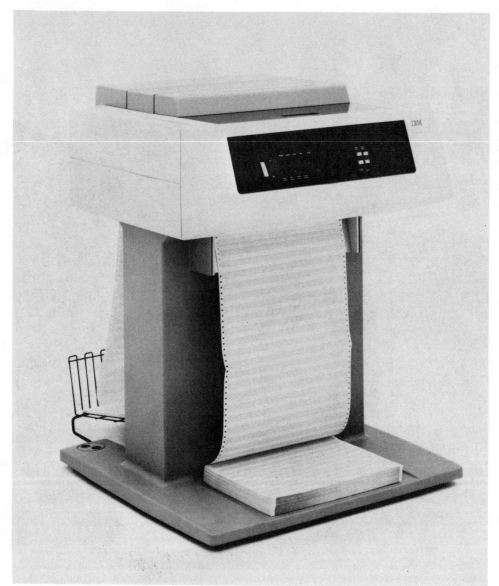

Figure 1-5 • IBM® 3268 Printer (courtesy of the International Business Machines Corporation)

often costing millions of dollars. Mainframe computers are invaluable to universities, large corporations, and federal agencies and in other situations that (1) collect or produce large amounts of information, (2) require rapid analysis of problems with complex or repetitive solutions, and (3) have many users.

The Minicomputer

The minicomputer is smaller, both in physical size and in its capabilities, than the mainframe computer. (See Figure 1-6.) It is often used to collect and process information from data acquisition systems in laboratories and for record keeping in medium-size companies. A minicomputer has a smaller memory capacity (typically several hundred thousand to a few million memory storage locations) and can usually handle fewer devices like terminals and printers than can mainframe computers. The minicomputer is often capable of supporting two or more persons simultaneously. Its operating speed may be slower than a mainframe computer. The environment of the minicomputer may not be as strictly controlled as that of the mainframe. The price range of a typical minicomputer is from $30,000 to $250,000.

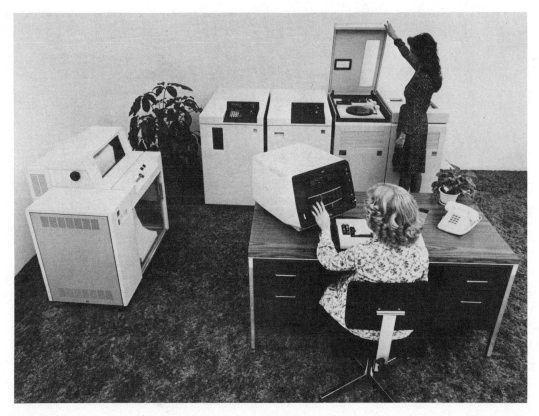

Figure 1-6 • IBM® 8100 Information System (courtesy of the International Business Machines Corporation)

The Microcomputer

The microcomputer is the smallest in terms of capabilities of the three classes of computers. (See Figures 1-7 through 1-9.) It is the slowest (perhaps only a tenth as fast as the minicomputer), supports the fewest peripherals (printers, storage devices, etc.), is the most limited in the size of numbers and arrays of numbers it can handle, and is usually the least expensive. Many microcomputers will allow only one person at a time to use them. The microcomputer's price range is from less than $1,000 to perhaps $20,000. The bulk of the material in this book is written with the microcomputer in mind.

Even though the microcomputer is slow and limited in its capabilities when compared with large computers, it is a very useful and valuable tool when the task is matched with the machine. Keep in mind that *slow* is a relative term. A slow microcomputer may perform only a

Figure 1-7 • Radio Shack TRS–80® Model II Microcomputer (courtesy of Radio Shack, a division of the Tandy Corporation)

Figure 1-8 • Radio Shack® Microcomputer with External Hard Disk Drive (courtesy of Radio Shack, a division of the Tandy Corporation)

Figure 1-9 • Osborne™ 1 Portable Computer (courtesy of the Osborne Computer Corporation)

Figure 1-10 • Hewlett-Packard HP–75 Hand-held Microcomputer with Two-pen Plotter (courtesy of the Hewlett-Packard Company)

few thousand operations per second, which is much slower than many of the mainframe computers, but is considerably faster than a human being. Microcomputers are becoming more and more commonplace in small businesses and laboratories. They are "personal" computers. An entire system can be located on a person's desk and used whenever it is convenient. Many of the new microcomputers can be carried in a brief-case or even in one's pocket (see Figures 1-10 through 1-12). Some of the microcomputer's most important advantages are accessibility, low turn-around time, and low overhead.

Figure 1-11 • Plotting Graphics with a Hewlett-Packard HP–41C/CV Hand-held Computer (courtesy of the Hewlett-Packard Company)

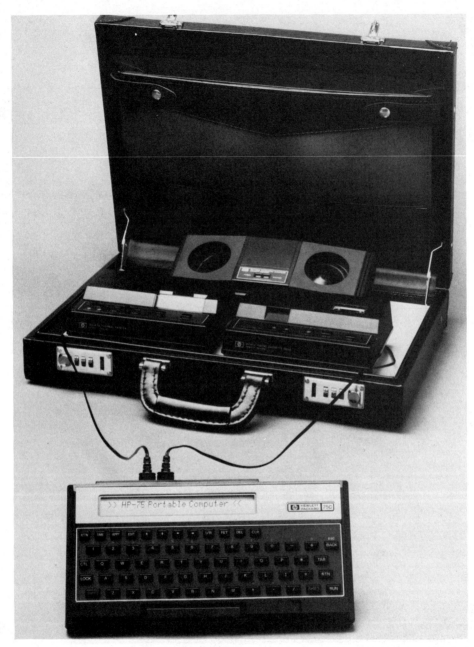

Figure 1-12 • Briefcase Microcomputing System with Computer Printer, Digital Cassette Drive, and Acoustical Coupler (courtesy of the Hewlett-Packard Company)

Advantages of the Microcomputer

Accessibility

The only way to learn how to use a computer is to actually use it. Reading about a computer's functions and how it works is a good place to begin, but actual practice with a computer, or hands-on experience, is essential. You can read the principles of how a bicycle operates and watch others ride a bicycle, but you will never be able to ride a bicycle until you actually get on one and suffer a few spills. Learning how to use a computer is very similar to riding a bicycle, including taking a few spills along the way. It is in the actual use of the machine that one learns how it works and what it will do. And the more you use it, the more proficient you become with it.

Most microcomputing systems are designed to be used by only one person and will fit on top of a small desk or table. If the computer is at your desk, it is definitely accessible. The more accessible the computer is, the more likely you are to use it.

Accessibility can be judged by how easy the equipment is to use. If something is very difficult to learn, it becomes, in effect, inaccessible. Most microcomputers do not incorporate such features as passwords and account numbers, which are often found on large computing systems. People are seldom charged for computer time on microcomputers. It is relatively easy to switch the microcomputer from one kind of task to another. Changing from a crop records program to a statistical analysis package to an electronic spread sheet is usually a simple matter of inserting a different diskette into a disk drive. Simpler user procedures and greater control over the system make the microcomputer easier to use and more accessible than mainframe computers.

Large computers require full-time programmers and operators devoted to making the computer work. It may take several days for a user to become proficient with the system. The basic operation of most microcomputers can be learned in a few hours. Many microcomputers are ready to run in the BASIC language as soon as they are turned on. Operators need little understanding of computers to use many of the programs available to them. For example, the word processing computer program used in writing this book came with a set of audio cassette tapes and two instruction books. The cassettes provided step-by-step instructions in nontechnical terms for using the word processor, and I was able to begin using the program with confidence in less than two hours after I began.

Fast turnaround time

In computer jargon, *turnaround* refers to the time between when a person gives the computer a program to run and when he receives the results. A large computer with several users may have a turnaround time of a day or more, depending upon the demand by the other people using it and the priority assigned to your particular task. When a program is given or "submitted" to a large computer, it is usually placed in a queue with several other programs or "jobs," which means several other programs must be run before yours. (A queue is a line. Your job has to wait in line until its turn.) This can be a frustrating and inefficient process when the results are needed immediately or when you are developing a new program.

Simple programming changes can mean long delays. If the turnaround time is one day, several days may elapse before one could debug a program and obtain useful results. Because of experiences like these with large computers, many people have become disillusioned with all computers and have simply quit using them altogether.

The microcomputer eliminates the turnaround time problem. It is right there beside you when you need it, and it is under your control. You do not have to wait for it to finish someone else's programs before it does yours. Programming mistakes can be found quickly and corrected and the program can be rerun right away. Programming alternatives can be tried and analyzed while the information is still fresh in the user's mind. If one has to wait hours or days between each run, a lot of thought continuity is lost.

The microcomputer can be used in the laboratory. If some experiments are being performed, the scientist can quickly analyze the results of a test and make changes in the experimental setup without having to wait hours to discover the results are invalid and the test needs to be repeated.

Up-to-date statistics

Good management of a business requires current records. It is just as important for small businessmen to keep up with their inventory, labor and sales records as it is for the large company. Reports that are one or two months old may be good historical records for a business, but they are not useful in making day-to-day decisions. Some small businesses mail their records to a computer facility at another location. By the time they receive the results, it may be too late to properly react.

A microcomputer with sufficient memory, storage capacity, and the proper software can provide the current status whenever it is needed. A personal computer located in a parts department could provide immediate information on availability of parts on hand, their locations, and demands for various parts. It could supply daily or weekly reports on inventory, most profitable items, and other information necessary to efficiently manage a parts department.

Disadvantages of the Microcomputer

Although the microcomputer is a very versatile tool, it does have some disadvantages when compared with mainframe computers.

Support

The full-time operators and programmers who are necessary with a mainframe computer are very knowledgeable about the capabilities of the machine and can generally help users with whatever problems they may have in using the system. The microcomputer user has gained additional access to the machine, but has lost this support structure of individuals intimately acquainted with the system. When problems arise, it may be difficult to find answers.

Expansion capability

As an enterprise grows, its computing needs will also increase. Many microcomputers have very limited expansion capabilities and may become a hindrance when additional demands are placed on them. A second terminal may need to be added so that two people have access to the same data (inventory, shipping, accounts receivable, etc.). Additional memory may be needed to handle larger, more sophisticated programs. If a business grows beyond the capabilities of a particular microcomputer system, transferring the information to a larger system can be a very time-consuming and complicated process, in addition to the added equipment expenses. The expansion capabilities of a system should always be considered when selecting the best one for a given situation.

Storage

The microcomputer cannot handle very large data sets well. Most microcomputers do not have mass storage devices with enough capacity to store large data bases such as weather records for a state, student records for a university, or a complete parts inventory for a large hardware store. Even if the mass storage is available, the microcomputer's memory and computational speed are often inadequate for the task to be performed quickly.

Service

Equipment repair and maintenance can be difficult with microcomputer systems. The cost of service contracts is often quite high in relation to the cost of the equipment, and the equipment usually has to be returned to a service center for repair.

Data sharing

It is harder to share data with other users when using a microcomputer. Large computing systems are set up to allow remote accessing. They can usually store data and programs on large reels of magnetic tape, which can be formatted for use by other computers. Microcomputers do not lend themselves well to remote accessing by other computers, and there are many incompatible formats for the disks and tapes used by the different systems. For example, an IBM Personal Computer® cannot read disks from a Radio Shack® computer, which in turn cannot read Apple® disks, which in turn cannot use Atari® disks, which in turn cannot read Osborne® disks, etc.*

Speed

Microcomputers are much slower than mainframe computers. For example, a cotton harvesting simulation program developed in our department last year took over two hours to run on a microcomputer, and less than one minute on the mainframe computer.

The microcomputer will never replace the large computer. Both have their own strengths and weaknesses. It is up to each user to use the system best suited for the particular task.

---

*The IBM Personal Computer® is a registered trademark of International Business Machines, Inc. Radio Shack® is a registered trademark of the Tandy Corporation. Apple® is a registered trademark of Apple Computer, Inc. Atari® is a registered trademark of Atari, Inc. Osborne™ is a trademark of the Osborne Computer Corporation.

Do Computers Make Mistakes?

A BASIC language program consists of a series of statements which contain instructions for the computer to follow. In most forms of BASIC, the instructions are divided into lines with one or more instructions per line. Each line must begin with an integer number, usually in the range from 0 to 65536. The computer performs the instructions from left to right in each line and from the lowest line number to the highest line number. The line numbers are not part of the instructions, but they determine the order in which the instructions are performed. The line numbers do not have to follow any particular sequence, but many program writers will start with line number 10 or 100 and number the following lines in increments of ten. Incrementing by ten allows up to nine more lines to be inserted later between each present line number. This is done in case an instruction was omitted or additional instructions need to be included.

A computer will always perform as instructed unless there are electronic failures within it. It will give the same result every time it performs the same operation (addition, subtraction, sorting, counting, etc.). This does not mean that it will perform as you think it will or should or as you want it to perform. Erroneous results produced by a computer are usually the result of the programmer not programming the computer correctly or of a user giving the computer wrong information. Computer people sometimes refer to this latter situation as "garbage in-garbage out."

Sometimes what seems to be a mistake is really a lack of understanding about what is happening in the computer program. Consider the following BASIC program:

```
10 FOR I = 1 TO 10
20 J=J+I
30 NEXT I
40 PRINT J,I
50 END
```

The first statement in this program, line 10, tells the computer to set a variable quantity labelled "I" to a value of one and to execute statement 20 ten times. Line 20 tells the computer to replace the value of a variable quantity labelled "J" with its previous value plus the present value of I. In most computer languages, including BASIC, the equals sign (=) means "replace the value of the variable on the left hand side of the statement with the quantity on the right hand of the statement." It does not mean "is equal to." That is, the equals symbol is used to assign the value of an expression to a variable rather than to denote equality between two expressions. Statement 20 is therefore a valid computer statement even though it is not a valid algebraic equation (unless I happens to be equal to zero).

When statement 30 is reached, the value of I is incremented by one, the program returns to the first statement following the FOR statement (line 10), and the process continues until I has a value of 10. Lines 10 through 30 comprise a FOR/NEXT loop. That is, the program "loops" between these two statements until variable I reaches or exceeds its upper limit. The last time through the loop, I has a value of 10. After the loop is completed, line 40 is executed and the values of J and I are printed. The program stops or ends when it reaches line 50. You cannot tell what values will be printed for J and I without knowing how your particular computer handles this type of operation.

In the loop (lines 10 – 30), some machines will increment I first and then compare the resulting value with the limit of the loop (in this case 10), before making a decision whether to loop or to continue to the next line in the program. In these cases, the value printed for I would be 11. Other machines will check the value of I before incrementing to see if it should go back to the beginning of the loop. In this second situation, the value printed for I would be 10.

Now consider the variable J. It would be "reasonable" to expect it to have a value of $1+2+3+ \ldots +10 = 55$. In some machines, 55 would be the value printed, because J was assumed to have an initial value of zero. In other computers, an error would occur the first time line 20 was reached because J was never explicitly assigned an initial value, so the program would not run. In these cases, another line would have to be inserted before line 10 to define $J = 0$.

Remember that the point of this example was to show the necessity for understanding how the computer works to make it do what you wish. It may seem like a lot of explanation for such a simple program, but understanding such details is necessary to do your own programming.

Statements such as, "What it is supposed to do is . . . ," "What I mean is . . . ," and "Basically, what I want is . . ." have no meaning in the world of computers. Computers cannot reason. If a computer was keeping track of the amount of grain in a storage bin, it would not consider a 20,000 bushel bin to be empty if it still had one kernel in it, whereas, a person would consider it to be empty. Computers make few assumptions, and the ones they make are probably not what you want them to be. Computers are very stupid—they have to be told every little detail about what they are expected to do. They are extremely finicky—a misplaced comma in a program can keep the program from running. However, their redeeming features more than compensate for their shortcomings. They are fast, accurate, always available, and untiring—endless repetition does not bother them at all.

Writing a Computer Program

Because of necessity or interest, many computer users write at least some of their own programs. There may be no programs on the market that will do exactly what you need to be done, or you may not be able to afford one that will do what you want. Be careful about not buying a program because it is expensive and you think you can write your own more cheaply—it is very easy to underestimate the cost of developing your own software. Most programs take at least twice as long to write as the most pessimistic time estimate.

Learn the language

To write a computer program, one needs to know the computer's language. If you cannot "speak" the computer's language, you cannot make it understand what you want. A computer language is a set of statements, commands, and relationships that the computer can understand and perform. Few of the languages used by microcomputers can be used on other microcomputers without modifications. The second computer may print a little differently, its display screen may not be able to contain as many characters, its graphics capabilities may be greater or less than the first, or it may store and retrieve programs and data differently.

One of the best ways to learn a computer language is to take a course offered by the computer store where the computer was purchased. That way you learn the idiosyncrasies of the language as it applies to your particular machine. If such a course is not offered locally, a second option is to acquire a tutorial program that teaches the language. A tutorial program usually consists of an instruction book and a set of cassette tapes with audio instructions. Others have program disks or tapes that can be used with your computer. In the latter case, the computer itself can teach you its language (or languages). It is best to use a tutorial written specifically for your system. A third option is to read a book on the language. A fourth choice is to enroll in a course that teaches the language in a general way, such as those offered by a community college or other institution. The language syntax may not exactly match that of your machine, but a great deal can still be learned from the course.

Regardless of the method chosen to learn a computer language, the most important factor is practice. Practice, practice, practice! No language can be mastered without actual experience using it. The commands and operations are quickly forgotten unless they are used. The more one uses a language, the more efficient and refined his programming skills become.

Steps in writing a computer program

If you decide to write your own software, certain steps must be followed to write a "good" program. What constitutes a good program will become apparent when you study the steps in writing one.

Rule 1. Define the problem. (1) I need a program to balance my checkbook. (2) My business needs an inventory control program.

Rule 2. Define the results needed and the form they should take. It is very important to have the results in a form that requires as little additional explanation as possible for the person who will be using them.

The checkbook program should provide a list of all check numbers, payee, amount of check, date on which check was written, and dates and amounts of deposits. The checks should be listed in ascending numerical order with the payee and amount of check on the same line with the check number. Deposits should be listed separately.

The inventory control program should provide a weekly listing of all part numbers, descriptions, quantities on hand, and number of units sold within the last week. The listing should be in order of number of units sold, with the item with the largest number listed first. The same listing ordered by part number should be available as an option.

Do not require results that will not be useful in solving the problem. The more that is demanded from a program, the more complex it becomes, and the longer it takes to write. If the program will be used extensively, the extra programming time may be justified. If the added results are only of marginal value, the extra time required to write the program may not be justified.

Rule 3. Determine what information the program needs to have entered by the user. For the checkbook program, the operator will have to enter the date the check was written, check number, payee, amount of check, and date and amount of deposits. The original balance must be known.

For the inventory control program, it is necessary to enter the part number and the number sold, and possibly the selling price. The computer will need to already contain the beginning inventory and a description corresponding to each part number. There must be provisions for adding to inventory and for recording the cost of each item.

Rule 3 is very important—do not rush through it. Each step is designed to help develop the kind of program that will be of maximum benefit to the user. As the necessary inputs are defined and the desired results are formulated, the program requirements begin to expand. In the case of the inventory program, it became apparent that a way was needed to add to inventory and that it would be necessary to include the cost of the items. It might also be helpful if the program could point out which items were the most profitable.

Rule 4. Define the data, formulas, and other relationships that the program must contain. The checkbook program must contain the beginning balance, subtract the amount of checks from the balance, and add deposits to the balance.

The inventory program must contain a description for each part number, the cost of each item, and the beginning inventory.

Rule 5. Recheck existing software for something that will meet your needs. After you have carefully and explicitly stated what you need a program to do, it is possible you will realize that some existing program will do what you want, or at least the most important part. A few commercial programs are written to allow you to make modifications in them to meet your particular requirements, but most of the programs you can purchase are difficult or impossible to modify. The reason for stressing the use of existing software is that PRODUCTIVITY IS NOT INCREASED BY WRITING COMPUTER PROGRAMS; IT IS INCREASED BY USING THEM! Some people like to write their own programs, but that may not be the most efficient or economical approach.

Rule 6. Estimate the time required to write the program, then double it. Estimating the time needed to develop a working program only comes with experience. It seems like problems always arise that were never anticipated. Programs with many lines of code may take an hour of programming time for each 10 to 20 program lines. Experience may be the best teacher, but even then it is not easy to estimate programming time.

Will the need for the program still be there by the time you have written it? It is seldom worthwhile to write a program to perform a task only once. It will usually require less time to solve the problem by some other means if the problem only needs to be solved one time. A building contractor building one house probably could monitor the construction progress, supply availability, and timeliness of performing various tasks more easily without a computer than he could develop a program to do all of this for him. But, if several houses were being built simultaneously, a computer program could be a definite asset to his business. A computer is usually better than manual methods for performing the same task many times, or when there is a need to perform several similar tasks. It is often faster than manual methods, and less error prone since humans tend to make more mistakes when performing repetitious tasks.

Rule 7. Write the program.

Make a flowchart.   The flowchart is a block diagram showing how the computer program flows between steps (see the sample shown in Figure 1-13). Beginning programmers tend to omit the flowchart because it just seems like busywork. They plunge into writing the code with the assumption that once the requirements of the program are defined, it is a simple task to write the program to do the job. With simple programs (fewer than 30 or 40 lines of instructions), a flowchart is usually unnecessary. However as a program becomes more complex, the coding becomes increasingly difficult, and a good flowchart is the only way for the programmer to keep up with what the program is doing. Unless the program is very short, DRAW THE FLOWCHART!!

Write in modules.   Divide the program into sections or modules, with each section performing a single task or set of related tasks. One module might set a value for, or initialize, the variables, another could print the results, a third could perform the calculations, and a fourth could input information from the operator. Understanding how a program operates and fixing its problems is easier when it is written in modules.

DOCUMENT, DOCUMENT, DOCUMENT!   Documenting a program means including remarks in the program listing itself to explain what the program is doing. If the program is a very complex one to use, written instructions should also be prepared. Some of the programs that have been developed in our department by some of the faculty are very sophisticated and very useful for the students. However, they are useless to many of the students because there are no written instructions on how to use them. Even the students who understand programming cannot use them because the program listings do not have any comments that explain what the code is doing. Remarks should be included in a computer program for the person reading the program, not for the computer. A well-documented program listing enables a person to read and understand what the program is supposed to be doing.

    Good documentation is necessary for two reasons. The first reason is that other people may need to modify the program at a later date. It is extremely difficult to understand someone else's program unless it is well documented. It is often easier to rewrite a program from scratch than it is to take someone else's program that has no comments and modify it. The second reason for documenting a program is to allow you to change your

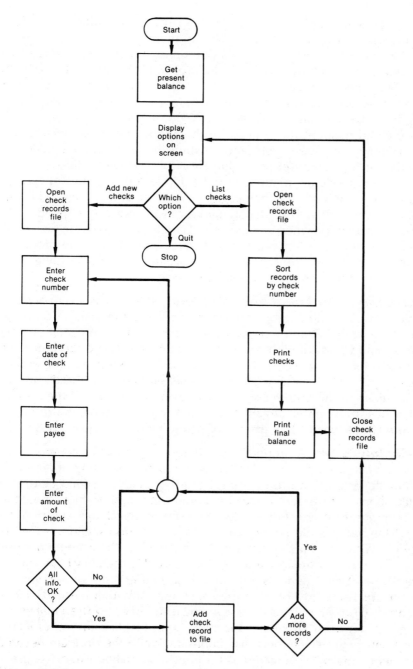

Figure 1-13 • Flowchart for Checkbook Program

own program. It is difficult to understand your own undocumented programs six months after you have written them.

Problems or mistakes in a computer program are called "bugs." You "debug" a program by correcting the problems. A problem could be the type that causes the computer to stop running because it was unable to perform an instruction. Or it could be a mistake where the program might run without any indicated errors, but the answers are wrong. The latter could happen, for example, if the wrong conversion factors were used, or two numbers were added when they should have been subtracted, or the computer was using data from the wrong file.

Program documentation should begin as the first lines of code are written. Do not wait until the program is finished and debugged to document it. While it is true that remarks will decrease the speed of the program execution when an interpreted language is used, the time differential will not be noticeable except in large programs. If the program is running too slowly, you can always remove the comments. However, do not remove them unless it is really necessary.

Make the output neat and complete. If the answer is in dollars, a $ placed before the number will make understanding easier. Control the format to fit the situation. If an answer is in dollars and cents, only two digits should be printed to the right of the decimal. Some computers may print several digits past the decimal point unless instructed differently by the program. An answer of $1,234.56 is better than 1234.559999. Any sets of numbers in the output should include an explanation. If the program calculates the number of gallons of paint required to paint a room, the output should read "17.5 gallons of paint" rather than just "17.5."

Write logically. A properly written flowchart makes a computer program much easier to write. Generally, the program listing order should follow the execution order. If a set of input data is needed before any calculations can be performed, then either the input section should appear before the calculation section, or a statement calling a subroutine to input the data should be included in the calculation section. If the program is written with an interpreted form of BASIC, the listing order does not have to follow the execution order. A BASIC program will usually run faster when the statements are put in descending order of use, with the statements used most often at the beginning. Although it is important in theory to write statements in descending order of use with an interpreted language, in most situations the user cannot notice the difference in execution time. It only becomes important when the program becomes very long (maybe several hundred lines), or makes extensive use of subroutines.

Program line numbers should always be in ascending order, with the lowest numbered line at the beginning of the program. Some languages like FORTRAN permit lines to be numbered in any order. However, random line numbering makes understanding the program very difficult.

Make it friendly.   Instruction manuals are often helpful, but a good program should require as little referral to the manual as possible. If the operator is confused or needs more information, a good program may even provide additional "helps" or explanations of commands when asked. A friendly program tells the person using the computer what is expected of him, and what form his response should take. If a question requiring a yes or no answer is asked, then state the type of response expected. This could take the form of "Do you wish to continue? (Y or N)" or "Do you wish to continue? (yes or no)."

In complicated programs, allow for the possibility that the wrong kind of data may be entered. In the example in the preceding paragraph, what would happen if the user responded with "not yet" or "wait?" (In simple programs, it may be easier to rerun the program than to build in extensive error-checking routines.) If a "yes" or "no" answer is expected, what happens if someone answers "maybe?" If a number such as "2" is expected, will something fail if the reply is "two?" Have the program check for errors in the input whenever possible. What if a program was supposed to keep track of how much time Sam Jones spent working on different pieces of machinery, and it asked how many hours were spent on the yellow tractor, and the user responded with "7 hours?" If the program does not detect this as an illegal entry, it may have an error in execution or produce meaningless results.

When the computer wants a response from the operator, it should explain what kind of response it is expecting. For example, if it needs to know the width of a building, the screen should print a message such as "Enter width of building in feet." If the units (in this case, feet) are not specified, the operator may enter inches, or meters, or yards. While this is valid input as far as the program is concerned, the answer will be wrong and there will be no indication that there is an error.

Rule 8. Debug and validate.   After the program is written, try as many kinds of test cases as possible. Make certain that it can handle improper responses. Does it give the right answers for a known set of inputs? Is it as flexible as you need it to be? Does the output look "nice?" If other people will be using your program, it will be judged on its ease of use, the neatness and readability of its output, and the accuracy of the results (and quite often in that order of importance).

Summary

Now that you have been given an introduction to the world of computers, we are ready to proceed to some guidelines for selecting a computer system for your particular needs.

Chapter 2
How to select a computer system

This chapter addresses the question of how to select a computer system. The choice of the term *system* is deliberate. Your goal should always be to select the proper system, which is comprised of both the computer software and the hardware. The computer is helpless without the software to give it instructions, and the software is worthless without the hardware. And neither one is any good unless it helps you with your problems. Your concern is to find the combination of hardware and software to meet your specific needs.

Selecting the wrong computer system can cause hard feelings and frustration, as well as wasted money and effort. The student who asked me what to do with the $25,000 computer his father had just purchased for their farming operation was frustrated. They had been told all of the wonderful things that the computer could do for them, but no one had mentioned that someone had to write the programs to make it do these wonderful things. The father was upset because he had spent a lot of money and all he could do with his computer was play Star Trek. One of my neighbors recently spent several thousand dollars on a computer system for his business. After using it a short time, he discovered that it would cost $1,000 for any modifications in his software, and the data in the program needed to be changed every one to two months to keep up with the changes in his business. In both of these cases, the buyers felt their computers were a waste of time and money, and, for their situations, they were right.

Selecting the right computer system can save money and time and increase productivity. Another farmer recently used a computerized farm analysis program to evaluate renting additional land and purchasing additional equipment. In less than two hours of his time, he found a way to increase his profits over $40,000. The difference in these situations was whether or not the system lived up to the seller's promises and the buyer's expectations and needs.

There are three steps that will help in selecting the right computer system for you:

1. Define your needs.
2. Select the software to meet those needs.
3. Select the hardware required for the software chosen.

Let's examine these three steps a little more closely.

Define Your Needs

Establish your requirements—both present and future—in as much detail as possible. How large is your operation? Determining this will help you decide how many records will need to be kept. What kind of statistics do you need generated? Do you need charts, or financial statements? How about payroll records? Is there a need to compute income taxes and payroll deductions? Do you anticipate adding farm land? Do you need a method to protect some records so that only selected individuals can modify them (salary records, inventories, hours worked, etc.)? Do you need a way of maintaining production records for livestock or cropping enterprises? If so, how many categories do you need for the livestock and the crops? How much and what kind of information do you need to record for these enterprises? Do you need a method for maintaining an inventory? How many parts, and what kind of descriptions are needed? Will all parts of the same kind be priced the same? Do you need a reorder notification when parts (or feed or fertilizer) get below a certain level? Don't skim over this step lightly. Examine your situation and requirements as thoroughly as possible, since what you will purchase depends upon this analysis.

Once you identify and quantify your requirements, you are ready to select the software.

Select the Software

Select the software to meet the needs you have identified. Talk to other people using computers in similar enterprises. Find out what kind of experiences they have had. Ask them what kind of help they received when they had problems. Talk with some users' groups. A users' group is a group of people that use a particular brand of computer, or a particular type of software, and meet to discuss common problems and interests. These groups often include people knowledgeable in both software and hardware and in fixing some of the problems that inevitably develop. Read some computer magazines. Several of them publish evaluations on a wide range of computer programs and equipment. Talk to some computer salesmen. The good ones are interested in helping you find the system that is best for you.

There are several difficulties you should be aware of when you purchase computer programs. The biggest problem is that a software package can be very well written, be clearly documented, be easy to use, and function properly and still be of no value to the user because it does not do what is really needed.

Suppose you buy an inventory control program that has been highly recommended by people you trust. These people used it and found it would do everything they needed. It was easy to use, everyone liked it, and it saved hours of record keeping. Based upon their reactions, you buy the program and assume it will do the same for you. Then you find out it can only handle 10-digit part numbers, and all of your parts have 11-digit identifications. Or, you find out it cannot provide listings sorted according to the number of items sold, and that is the feature you really need. Your associates never needed those capabilities, so they thought the program was fine. You do need those features, so you are stuck with an expensive program that is of no value to you unless you make undesirable changes in your procedures to suit the computer.

What kind of changes will you need to make in your procedures or record keeping to use the software? It may be worthwhile to make certain changes to use an otherwise acceptable computer program. For example, you may customarily enter dates as the day followed by the month followed by the year. A particular program may expect the date to be in the form of month, day, and year. In this kind of situation, the simplest thing to do may be to change the way you record dates. Other situations may require major changes in your operating procedures. What if the program does all of its calculations with kilograms and hectares, and you work with acres and bushels, or vice versa? If a major change in your operating methods is required to use a particular software package, it might be best to consider using other software more suited to your needs. The computer was made for man—man was not made for the computer.

Another potential problem with buying computer programs is that there is still software on the market that is not worth the floppy disk on which it is written. Software may contain errors, may be difficult to use, may come with documentation that is skimpy or hard to understand, or may not include documentation. The software vendor may not provide any training or support and may feel any problems you have are definitely your problems and not his. While the number of programs in this second category is rapidly diminishing from the market, inferior quality products will always exist. It is the buyer's responsibility to make certain he does not get stuck with some of it.

Will the software you are considering do all of the special things you need it to do? Will it do them in its present form? Are you sure?

Some operations have peculiar requirements and general-purpose programs may or may not be able to handle your particular situation. A farmer may have different requirements for an accounting system than have other small businessmen. This is not the time to take the saleperson's word for too many things without proof. Have the salesperson demonstrate the package's capabilities. If he says he knows it can be done, but he just does not know how to do it, be leery!

One salesperson told us that his computer could communicate as a remote terminal with a large computer located elsewhere, but he could not demonstrate it because he did not have the necessary telephone modem. Weeks after we purchased the computer, we discovered that it could indeed be done, but only with several weeks of programming on our part, and in a computer language that we did not know.

The software you are promised may be ready in two weeks, or it may be ready in two years. Estimating how long it will take to develop a complex computer program is very difficult. Perfecting programs (if that is really possible) takes time, and the more complicated the program, the longer the process takes. Bugs are a problem—a bug is a problem in the software that causes it to give incorrect answers or do something else wrong. Many large computer programs contain bugs that are not discovered until after the programs have been on the market for a while. This occurs either because the software writer hurried to release the program to meet a deadline and was not thorough in checking it or because the user tried to make the program do something for which the developer did not plan. When the first mailing list programs were written, who suspected that more than five digits would ever be needed for a zip code?

The buyer should also be cautious when the salesperson promises that "the software will have *that* capability in a couple of weeks, it just hasn't been announced yet" or "We will give you the update as soon as we get it." We have been waiting over six months for programs that were ready for "immediate shipment upon receipt of order."

What kind of support can you get? It is not realistic to expect much help with a $20 checkbook balancing program, but it is reasonable to ask for a contact person to help with problems when using a $3,000 general accounting program.

Is the program guaranteed? What if there are bugs in the program and it will not perform as promised? Much of the software sold now is on an "as is" basis with the vendor assuming no responsibility for mistakes. However, some vendors will ensure that their products are properly installed and operating on your equipment. Product support is just as important with computer software and equipment as it is with just about anything else one purchases. But computers and their programs are often more difficult to fix than are many other products.

What about backup copies of the software? Some software comes on a disk that cannot be copied and the original diskette (or other recording media) cannot be duplicated. The original copy must always be used. The philosophy behind making a program uncopyable is to protect the software author and the vendor from the buyer making illegal copies and giving them away or selling them. However, if an accident should happen to the original, and the user cannot make a backup copy, he is without a program. A computer power failure at the wrong time is all it takes to destroy all of the information on a disk. Unless you have a backup copy, you may be in for an unacceptable delay while waiting for the vendor to replace the original or sell you another copy. Even though many times a vendor will replace a destroyed diskette for a nominal fee, the time factor is still a problem. Most businesses would be seriously impaired if their computer were inoperable for two or three weeks. (If they aren't, they may not need it in the first place.)

The three most popular types of computer programs for microcomputers are electronic spread sheets, data base management systems, and word processors. All three of these classes have applications in many areas, including agriculture. Many of the portable computers have some version of all three programs included in the purchase price of the machine. Here are some suggestions to consider when choosing from these programs.

The electronic spread sheet

The development of the electronic spread sheet program has been claimed as the factor most responsible for selling so many microcomputers for business applications. Whether or not that is true, these programs are very popular. While VisiCalc®, by VisiCorp*, is probably the most well known electronic spread sheet, there are also several other versions on the market today.

The spread sheet consists of a two-dimensional matrix of rows and columns. (By the time this is in print, perhaps the rumored three-dimensional one will have been introduced.) Each matrix location is defined by a row and column and is referred to as a "cell." Cells can contain either text or numerical values. The text can consist of any desired letters or other characters, such as column titles. The numerical cells can contain either simple numbers or can be defined as a function of one or more of the other cells. For example, the seventh cell in the fourth column might be the product of the two adjacent cells in the same row or be defined as the sum of cells 2 through 6 in that same column.

Applications for electronic spread sheets in agriculture are increasing. These include calculating grain drying costs, financial statements, chemical applications, and production costs for crops and livestock operations.

The spread sheet is proving to be very useful in examining the effects of changes in an operation. This examination is sometimes referred to as a "sensitivity analysis." For example, the price of grain is an important factor in the profitability of a livestock finishing operation. But there are several other things to consider, including labor, housing, and medical expenses. A spread sheet could be developed to show the expected

---

*VisiCalc® is a registered trademark of Visicorp.

profit of a finishing operation as the grain prices varied throughout the year. Once the spread sheet has been defined, testing the impact of varying grain prices is a simple matter.

Grain marketing is influenced by storage capacity, storage costs, drying costs, market price, and interest rates. A spread sheet could be designed to calculate both the costs and the net profit for selling the grain at different times following harvest. One could quickly see the results of selling part of the grain immediately and holding the rest until a later date. Several schemes could be tested in a matter of minutes, once the initial spread sheet was developed.

How do you select a spread sheet? You want at least three things: ease of use, flexibility, and sufficient size for the task.

Ease of use.   How easy a piece of software is to use is a function of both the external and internal documentation. The external documentation consists of all the written materials supplied with the program. Sometimes the physical quality of the documents provides an indication of the quality of the program. Mimeographed instructions for an $800 spread sheet would make me a little wary about the quality of the software. While it is not necessarily a good indicator, it should not be ignored. Clear, complete instructions are important to have, particularly with sophisticated programs. If you do not understand how to use a program, the program is almost useless no matter how powerful it is.

Look through the instructions. Are they easy to read? Do you have to be a computer expert to understand the terminology? Are there examples illustrating all of the program's main features? Do they include samples of what the display should look like? Is there a good index? Are topics presented in a logical order? Is the documentation meant to serve as a reference book or as a tutorial to get you started using the program? Preferably, both kinds of information should be provided. A tutorial is useful when you are learning to use a new program, but it is usually a poor reference when you have a specific problem. Similarly, a reference book will help you answer specific questions, but it is not very useful when you are learning how to use the program.

After examining the manuals, load the program into the computer, make a few entries, and try some of the commands. If you get stuck, is there some kind of HELP feature that will explain your options without destroying the data you have entered? Do the explanations make sense? Is there a section of the display that always tells you where you are (which cell) in the spread sheet and what mode or type of operation you are performing? How easy is it to change information in a cell? Can the contents of a cell or a column or row be copied or moved to another location? Can selected cells be protected so they will not be accidentally deleted or changed while other cells are being changed? If you try to do something major, like erase the entire spread sheet or quit without saving what you have already done, does the program prompt you to make certain that is what you really intended to do? Sometimes it is easy to press the wrong key, and you want the computer to be tolerant enough to allow a simple mistake without producing catastrophic results.

Flexibility.   Flexibility really means can the program do what you need to have done. What kinds of modifications are allowed and are there assumptions the computer makes that cannot be changed? For example, does the computer always assume that the entire spread sheet has to be printed? What if your printer could not handle as many columns as the spread sheet? Could the printout be modified to take this into consideration? How many spaces are allowed in each cell? What if more text is needed in a cell than there are number of spaces available? What about accuracy?

How complex can the formulas be in a cell? Is exponentiation allowed? What about logarithms? Is it possible to "split the screen?" That is, can the spread sheet be split into sections so rows or columns in two different sections can be viewed simultaneously? Is it possible to display the information in a graphical form? If the program was being used to compute an enterprise's profit on a monthly basis, could it print a bar chart showing the profit for each month?

Sufficient size for the task.   What are the biggest and smallest numbers allowed? How many digits are used in calculations? Is that sufficient for your applications? How many columns and cells are available? Be sure to remember that if two computers are using spread sheet programs and one computer has more memory than the other, the one with the larger memory may not necessarily be able to handle more rows and columns. The limitations on the size of a spread sheet are governed by how the program itself was written, the language in which it was written, and the computer's memory. If a program cannot avail itself of more memory, the fact that the computer has it is of no benefit.

When considering spread sheets, remember that the results are only as reliable as the data and the relationships used. If your calculations showed that a 25 cents per bushel increase in price would double your profit, and you waited for the market to reach that price, which it never did, the analysis was not much help. If the formulas used in the spread sheet raised the yield 10 bushels per acre for each 30 pounds of nitrogen added, the answers would be invalid unless that is how the yield actually increased. An electronic spread sheet cannot provide you with any new information you could not find without it. It will only provide you with the same information previously available, but it will do it in less time. The main advantages of the faster information processing are the likelihood of fewer errors in calculations and the ease in studying the effects of changes in inputs (labor costs, rate of inflation, market price, more land, more equipment, etc.). The ability to quickly determine the effects of changes should encourage one to perform a more thorough analysis before making a decision.

The data base management system

A data base management system (DBMS) is a computer program, or set of programs, used to create, store, change, sort, and display one or more sets of data. The data is composed of a set of entries called "records." The records are stored as a group in a file on a cassette tape, a floppy diskette, or a hard disk. A DBMS can be very useful for storing information about an enterprise or several interrelated enterprises.

Consider the task of maintaining machinery use and fertilizer applications for a farming operation that includes cotton, soybeans, oats, and a pecan orchard. These crops are grown in 20 different fields. Machinery use records and fertilizer applications need to be maintained for each crop and each field, for the total machinery use for each implement, and for the total fertilizer application for each type of fertilizer.

Each record is made up of one or more parts called "fields." A field is a single piece of information within a record. In our example, some of the records would have fields for the name of the crop, the date, a crop field identification, kind of fertilizer, and the amount applied. Other records in the same file would have fields for the date, crop field identification, implement used, and the number of hours it was used.

Some of the record fields would be the same for the two record types and some would be different. Each record field is reserved for a particular type of information. One would be for the date, another for fertilizer type, a third for implement used, etc. Any one record would use some but probably not all of the fields.

Separating a record into fields enables the sorting of them in different ways. Records are sorted by listing them in numerical or alphabetical order or by separating them into groups based upon some characteristic of one or more of the record fields. Sorting might be by dates, implements, or application rates. It is also possible to sort within ranges within a field or by listing all fields whose entries exactly match one specified by the user. A range search might mean finding all records between two specified dates. A matching search could find all records related to the pecan orchard. A combination search and/or sort is possible, too. You could list all fertilizer applications on cotton, or all operations on the southwest section of land before May 10.

If a record field contains numerical data, it is possible to sum the field. For example, one could find the total amount of anhydrous ammonia used in the growing season, or the number of hours that tractor number 3 had spent disking the oats ground.

When selecting a DBMS, here are some features to consider:

1. Maximum record length.
2. Maximum number of records in a file.
3. Maximum number of unkeyed fields.
4. Number of keys allowed in searching and sorting.
5. Ability to add and delete fields after records have been created.

Record length and number of records.   The record length is the number of characters, including spaces, in a record. The maximum record length and the number of records in a file are interrelated. As the record length increases, the number of records allowed in a file decreases. These values should be examined closely. There are limits on the total length of individual records, and on the number of keyed and unkeyed fields. There is usually a limit on the length of any individual field.

Recently I was consulted on a medical records problem. A medical group had purchased a well-known DBMS for their microcomputer system. According to the manuals that came with the DBMS, up to 50,000 records could be stored in a single file. However, after including all of the information needed in each record for each patient, the maximum number dropped from 50,000 to 23. In addition, when the record formats were being defined and the limits of the program were reached, the whole program stopped without warning and destroyed all the data.

Record lengths and file storage are closely related. It is wise to know about how much information you need in each record to determine if a particular program meets your needs. The manuals accompanying the program should include the relationship between record lengths and file storage. (The one purchased for the medical records system had this information, but the group had not read it.)

Keyed and unkeyed fields.   Record fields are either keyed or unkeyed. A keyed field is one that can be used for sorting and searching. In our machinery use and fertilizer application example, we might make the crop type and machine two of the keyed fields. An unkeyed field is one that cannot be used for sorting. The fertilizer application rate or a comments section could be unkeyed fields if they would never be needed to sort records.

Record fields are separated into keyed and unkeyed fields because of data storage methods and program capacity. Due to the way the program stores the fields, placing some of the information into unkeyed fields usually permits more records to be placed in a file and allows more information to be placed into each record.

Number of keys allowed in searching and sorting. Some systems allow multiple field sorting and searching. This allows one to identify very specific sets of data. The relationships allowed in these searches refer to how a record field compares with a constant. For instance, finding all fertilizer applications that do not use anhydrous ammonia is a comparison of the keyed field containing the fertilizer type with the constant of anhydrous ammonia. In this case, the system would identify all of the specified fields that are not equal to the specified constant. One could also find all of them equal to a constant, or less than or greater than. Less than and greater than comparisons are used to examine numerical values or alphabetized information. A numeric field might be searched for all values between 20 and 300. The number of keys allowed in a search determine what kind of data sets can be identified. If a 3-key field search was allowed, for example, we could find all pesticide applications before May 10 on any crop except cotton. A 3-key field search capability would probably cover most users' requirements.

Ability to add and delete fields after records have already been created. This ability is one of the most important features of any data base management program. It is quite possible that you may need to add more information to a set of records in the future. For instance, you may need to identify which worker is performing a specific task. Or you may need to include another field for custom work.

You certainly would not want to start from the beginning and enter all of the previous information into a new file. You want a method for adding fields to an existing one. Some of the DBMS programs available today do not have this capability. If some key field information was no longer useful, you might want to remove it from the files to increase the allowable number of records in the file or to replace it with another field. If the DBMS program does not have the add and delete field feature, once the record format has been defined, you cannot change it without losing whatever information is contained in the file.

Selecting the DBMS that is right for you requires a careful study of the documentation. If possible, buy the manuals separately and read them closely before making your decision.

The word processor

Word processing is a very popular use for microcomputers, since almost everyone communicates with the written word. Processing words involves creating them, arranging their order, and placing them on paper or some other material in a desired form. The simplest form of a word processor is a piece of paper and a pencil. A more sophisticated processor has an eraser for making corrections.

An electronic word processor usually contains a keyboard for creating text, a screen for displaying the text, a computer with the appropriate software (computer program) for holding and manipulating the information, a printer for placing the words on paper, and a mass storage device (typically one or more diskette drives) for storing the created material for future use. The words are usually not printed on paper until the material is in its final desired form.

The difference between an electronic word processor (henceforth referred to simply as a "word processor") and other computer systems is the software used by them. A computer is a multipurpose device whose function at any given time is determined by the program controlling it. Word processing software enables the computer to process words rather than to maintain financial records, to make statistical analyses, to play games, etc. Many word processors on the market now that have been sold strictly as word processing devices are really general purpose computers which happen to contain only a word processing program. Sometimes these dedicated systems are more efficient in processing words than are general purpose computers with word processing programs. This is because the dedicated systems were designed to do only one task, and to do it very well.

An acceptable word processor should at least enable one to enter characters (words, numbers, spaces, and other symbols), correct mistakes, insert new information in the midst of previously existing material, store the text for later retrieval and use, and print the text in a desirable form. Some word processors will also check spelling. Some will print form letters with names and addresses in a mailing list. Let's examine some of the factors to consider in selecting a word processor for your particular application.

Versatility. Do you need a machine that will do other programming tasks as well as word processing? If report generation and letter writing are to be the word processor's sole use, some of the dedicated word processing systems may be worth considering. But, if other uses may be required of the system, be certain the appropriate software is available for that particular system to meet your needs. Do not assume that since the processor contains a computer you will be able to use other programs with it. Transferring programs from one computer to another is not always easy and quite often impossible.

Ease of use. How difficult is it to use the word processing program? Is there any tutorial information—demonstration programs, audio tapes, etc.? What kind of documentation comes with the program? Do you have to be a computer expert to read it? (You should not have to understand very much at all about computers to use a word processor.) Are the manuals easy to read? Do they have a good index? At least one of the manuals should be a reference manual rather than a tutorial document. A reference manual is one to which you can refer when you have a specific question about the program's operation or when a problem arises.

How about helps within the word processing program itself? If you have a problem, can you press a "HELP" key, or something similar, to get more explanatory information without destroying whatever document you are working with? How easy is it to make a backup copy of individual documents or an entire diskette? What happens if a mistake is made in the middle of a document—is it possible to destroy a document by accidentally pressing the wrong key? The word processor should let you recover from mistakes without destroying too much of the material you have created. Some systems allow you to create a backup copy of a document before you revise the original, so you can go back to the original version if you make too many mistakes.

Speed. Are you a fast typist? Some processors cannot keep up with fast typists. Try pressing several keys one after the other as rapidly as possible to see if the system can keep up with you without losing any letters. What happens if you are in the middle of a word and you reach the right edge of the typing area? You should be able to continue typing and have the processor move the entire word to the next line so no words are broken at the end of a line. This feature increases the typist's speed because it allows the user to concentrate on typing rather than on the margins. Hyphenation can usually be taken care of after all of the text is typed into the computer.

Spelling checkers. How is your spelling? Several of the word processing packages can be purchased with spelling checkers. After a document is typed and before it is printed, the spelling checker reviews every word for correct spelling. This is a very useful tool, but it will only correct certain kinds of mistakes. A spelling checker compares every word in your document with its own vocabulary. If it finds a word that does not match any words in its dictionary, the word in question is highlighted for the user to examine and to either modify or accept as is. Some of the spelling checkers will also allow the user to add words to their vocabulary. This is a very useful feature. For example, an agronomist who used many scientific plant names could add those names to the spelling checker's vocabulary.

A spelling checker cannot check grammar or whether or not a particular word is being used correctly. The sentence, "I are not two god of a speller," would be perfectly acceptable to a spelling checker, because each word in it is a valid, correctly spelled word.

The display.   You cannot fully evaluate computer software without also examining the hardware (the part of the equipment you can actually touch). Some word processing system features, such as the display, are a function of both hardware and software. However, since you are interested in the total performance of the word processing system, it is not important that you know whether a feature is the result of the equipment or of the computer program controlling the equipment. Your primary concern is whether or not the system will perform its task.

How does the display look? Are the characters on the display large enough and well formed enough to be read easily? How many columns and rows can be displayed on the screen? Are there fewer columns than on the forms or letters that you use? If so, it may be awkward to determine how the final printed version of the text will appear. Is that important to you? The more rows of text that can appear on the screen, the better the system is. The ideal display, in my opinion, would contain a full page of text in the form in which it would appear when printed.

What does the system do with superscripts and subscripts? Some word processors cannot handle them at all. Others can process them but cannot display them properly (that is, place them a fraction of a space above or below the text line). Many processors require that special characters be entered into the text to inform the computer and printer when the scripted text needs to be printed. These special characters may appear on the screen, but will not appear in the printed version of the text.

In addition to being able to print both subscripts and superscripts, the printer must be able to properly interpret the superscript and subscript commands sent by the computer. Not all printers can perform subscripting and superscripting, and not all those that can use the same special commands to identify the sub- or superscripted information. Some word processors allow the user to modify the printing section to send the different commands needed by different printers; others do not allow this. Compatibility problems between the computer and the printer can be minimized by using a computer, a word processing program, and a printer from the same manufacturer. However, the problems may not be totally eliminated. Have all of your requirements for a word processing system demonstrated before purchasing the system.

Select the Hardware

Select the hardware needed for the software chosen. After you have defined your needs, and have selected the programs (software) for these tasks, you are ready to select the computer hardware (see Figures 2-1 through 2-5). As previously mentioned, the hardware is that part of the

Figure 2-1 • Radio Shack® Model 16 Microcomputer 16-bit Microcompressor (courtesy of Radio Shack, a division of the Tandy Corporation)

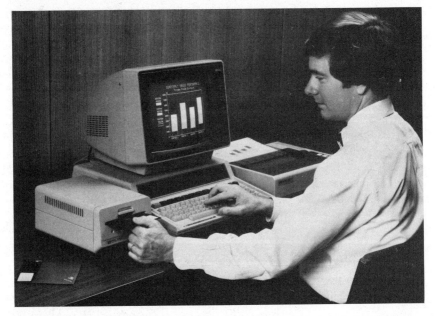

Figure 2-2 • Hewlett-Packard HP–86 Microcomputer System with Disk Drive, High-resolution Graphics Display, and Dot Matrix Printer (courtesy of the Hewlett-Packard Company)

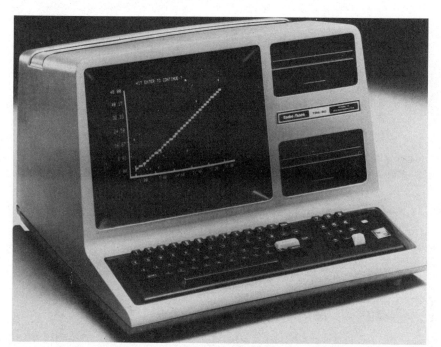

Figure 2-3 • Radio Shack TRS–80® Model III Microcomputer with Low-resolution Graphics (courtesy of Radio Shack, a division of the Tandy Corporation)

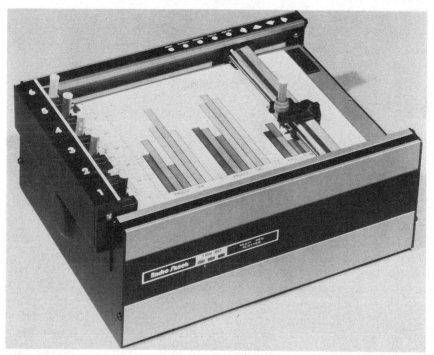

Figure 2-4 • Radio Shack TRS–80® Multi-pen Plotter (courtesy of Radio Shack, a division of the Tandy Corporation)

Figure 2-5 • Radio Shack TRS–80® Four-pen Plotter (courtesy of Radio Shack, a division of the Tandy Corporation)

computer and its accessories you can actually touch—keyboard, central processor, printer, screen, etc. The software you select automatically restricts your choice of hardware to whatever is needed to run the software. But, there may still be many choices or options to consider.

The display

A conventional television and a monitor both use a display device known as a CRT or cathode-ray tube. The CRT is an evacuated glass tube with a phosphor coating on the inside front surface. A stream of electrons is generated in the rear of the CRT and guided across the phosphor in closely-spaced horizontal lines. As the electrons hit the phosphor material, it begins to emit light. The intensity of the light is controlled by the number and speed of the electrons that hit any particular spot. By carefully guiding and controlling the stream of electrons it is possible to create letters, symbols, and pictures on the phosphor. In essence, the electron beam is used to draw the letters, symbols, and pictures with tiny dots of light. The color of the display is determined by the kind of phosphor used. Some phosphors emit green light, others red, or blue, etc. A CRT with only one kind of phosphor emits light of only one color and is used in a monochrome monitor or television. If three phosphors were used, one each of red, blue, and green, and they were placed in very

Figure 2-6 • Three Hewlett-Packard Display Sizes (courtesy of the Hewlett-Packard Company)

closely-spaced groups of three on the surface of the tube, and if each of the three phosphor types was hit by a separate electron beam, then it is possible to have a color display. The groups of three phosphor elements are so close together that the eye cannot separate the color produced by each of them, and their colors (which are the three primary colors) combine to produce any desired color, depending upon the relative light intensity produced by each of the three.

Some microcomputers can be connected to a conventional television by means of a device between the computer and the television called an RF modulator. An RF (radio frequency) modulator is a device that converts the computer's output signals into a form that can be transmitted through a television's antenna connector and displayed on the television. While this connection is satisfactory for games and occasional use, the image is not as sharp as that produced by a monitor. A monitor is similar to a television except that it does not have the extra circuitry necessary to translate television broadcast signals into a display image. (See Figure 2-6.) The monitor receives its signal directly from the computer hardware, and provides a sharper, clearer image than does a television. Other kinds of displays such as liquid crystal displays (LCDs) coming onto the market may soon provide options. They are potentially useful in portable computing systems because they permit the use of flat screens and a smaller, lighter unit.

The two main types of monitors to consider are color and monochrome cathode-ray tubes.

Monochrome monitors. Monochrome monitors generally come in black-and-white or green-and-white, with a few other colors also available. While many people prefer the green-and-white monitor, the choice may be a matter of personal preference. Examine different types before making a decision. Is the color pleasing to the eye? Could you look at it for hours without severe eye strain? Is there a lot of glare? The lights in a room can cause distracting reflections on a word processing screen just as they can on a television screen.

Color monitors. Color monitors are particularly useful in presenting graphical information. "Computer graphics" usually refers to lines, bars, and other symbols and pictures that are not part of the standard ASCII character set. Sometimes a graph or drawing communicates information much more effectively than do words. Pie charts can illustrate how money is divided among various enterprises. Line graphs show how profits have increased or declined over time. Bar charts can be used when comparing productivity of different countries or companies. Graphic displays are becoming more important as people become aware of their value.

When considering a color terminal, keep in mind that the only people who will be able to see the information will be the ones actually looking at the terminal. Will the graphic information be primarily for the user? If so, a color monitor may be a good investment. If many people need to see the information, make certain there is a good, convenient way to transfer the graphics to paper or film. Unless you can transfer the graphic display to paper or film, its effectiveness is greatly diminished.

Glare is probably a much greater source of operator fatigue and eyestrain than is the color of the display. Glare is a function both of how the monitor is made and of how it is placed in the room in relation to light sources. The screen should never be placed where bright lights can reflect from it into the eyes of the user. Some screens have an adjustable angle or tilt mechanism or provide a built-in or external glare reducing screen that is placed in front of the CRT.

The keyboard

Many computer systems come with one standard keyboard, so you must use it if that particular system is chosen. While most of the keyboards on the market seem to function well, you should remember several things when selecting one.

Do not get a membrane or flat keyboard or a calculator-style keyboard for serious computing. The membrane or flat keyboards are acceptable if typing is done only occasionally, but they are virtually useless for a touch typist. They are too slow for a serious word-processing environment. The calculator-style keyboard has keys similar to the ones on many of the pocket calculators. It is easier to use than the flat keyboard, but is not satisfactory for continuous use. Choose a keyboard with raised keys shaped and placed similarly to those on a conventional typewriter. Do the keys provide some kind of feedback when pressed? Many people prefer a small "click" when a key is depressed to assure them that the key was indeed activated. Can the keyboard be moved, or is it rigidly attached to the computer? Some keyboards attach to the computer with a flexible cord, which allows the keyboard to be moved a short distance from the processing unit.

Another important keyboard feature is a numeric keypad. A numeric keypad is a set of keys usually located in a cluster to the right of the regular keyboard. The keypad makes it much easier to enter numerical data. The data is entered much like numbers are entered on a calculator. The keypads are much more convenient and quicker than the regular keyboard. If your work includes a large amount of numerical entry, try to get a keyboard with the numeric keypad.

The printer

The two most common classes of computers used with microcomputer-based word processors are the dot matrix printer and the fully formed character printer. Other types of printers are thermal, ink-jet, and laser, but they are seldom used in microcomputer applications and will not be discussed here.

The primary factors to consider in a printer are the print quality, the printing speed, and the paper handling system. Printing quality of a dot matrix printer is partially determined as stated earlier by the matrix size. Another factor in determining quality is letters with "descenders." Do the small letters g, j, p, q, and y extend below the normal line of type, or are they even with it? Type is easier to read on printers that allow for descenders.

Printing speed is important. Printers are usually rated in characters per second or words per minute or by their baud rate. The first two rating methods are self-explanatory. To determine the number of characters per second from the baud rate, divide the baud by 10. The baud rate is a measure of how fast information can be transmitted. A baud rate of 300 is equivalent to 30 characters per second. The average printing speed of a printer is less than its rated speed. The rated speed is usually the maximum speed on a single line and does not include time to advance the paper or reposition the print head for the next line. You pay for printing speed. The higher the speed, the more costly the printer.

Paper handling needs to be considered. If individual sheets of paper are used, how are they fed into the printer? A conventional typewriter requires the typist to insert one sheet of paper, type the information on it, remove the sheet, insert another sheet, and start the process again. This is not very efficient with a word processor. A word processor is purchased to make the processing of words easier. If someone has to individually insert sheets of paper into the printer, the process becomes very inefficient. If your application requires the use of individual sheets of paper, and it is a large volume application, a paper sheet feeding device is worth considering. With this device, a stack of paper is placed in the feeder, and the paper is fed automatically into the printer as required. Sheet feeding devices are relatively expensive. On some printers, the sheet feeding device may cost as much as the printer.

A second kind of paper-feeding mechanism is the continuous form feeder. With this device the paper is supplied as a continuous stream of paper sheets that are connected by perforations. When the paper comes out of the printer, the sheets are torn apart at the perforations. Much of the continuous form paper also comes with holes punched in perforated strips along each side, which are used to accurately guide the paper through the printer. Some printers allow both kinds of paper to be used.

The dot matrix printer. The dot matrix printer contains a vertical row of circular metal pins (see Figure 2-7). As this row of pins moves horizontally across the paper, different combinations of the pins are

Figure 2-7 • Radio Shack TRS–80® DMP 2100 Dot Matrix Printer (courtesy of Radio Shack, a division of the Tandy Corporation)

struck and driven against a ribbon, which contacts the paper and creates the letters, numbers, and other symbols. The quality of the printing depends upon the number of pins used and the width of each character. A typical matrix printer might contain seven pins with each character formed with up to five horizontal positions. This allows the creation of symbols with a 5 by 7 matrix of pin positions or dots, hence the term *dot matrix printer*. The more pins used the higher the printing quality. A 7 by 9 matrix printer would have a higher quality output than would a 5 by 7 printer, for example.

The fully formed character printer. The fully formed character printer (sometimes called "letter quality") forms solid characters in a manner very similar to a typewriter (see Figure 2-8). Each character is fully formed on a round disk, wheel, or ball. One of the most popular types is the daisy wheel printer, which has the characters around the edge of a disk like petals on a daisy. When a character key is pressed, the appropriate character is rotated in front of the ribbon, and a small hammer-like device hits it and forms the character. Many people prefer the fully formed character printer over the dot matrix printer because the printing looks like typewriter printing.

Figure 2-8 • Radio Shack TRS–80® DWP 410 Daisy Wheel Printer (courtesy of Radio Shack, a division of the Tandy Corporation)

Which one is best? Matrix printers are very popular because many of them are cheaper than the daisy wheel printers. They are also faster. If your work requires "letter quality" printing (it looks like it was printed with a typewriter), a daisy wheel or other fully-formed character printer is necessary. Otherwise, a matrix printer is probably a better investment, since it usually offers more speed and flexibility for its cost.

How much memory?

When referring to a computer's memory one usually means the amount of electronic "space" the computer has to store programs and data. The smallest block of memory space is called a "byte." Each byte contains eight binary digits called "bits." Each bit can have a value of one or zero, so there are 256 unique possible values for a byte. Each symbol (letter, number, etc.) which the computer can understand is represented by one of these 256 byte values. Memory is usually specified in kilobytes, where one kilobyte is 1,024 bytes. A 48K computer would have $48 \times 1,024$ or 49,152 bytes of memory available for programs and data.

For computer-oriented people, there is no such thing as a computer with too much memory. They look at memory like boating people look at boats: the present boat is not quite as good as one that is just a little bigger. The computer person could always use a little more memory. More memory will allow the use of bigger programs, bigger arrays, and more data. For many of the 8-bit microcomputers, I would recommend getting the maximum memory configuration available for them. If it is 48K, get it. If it is 64K, get that. Many of the commercial software packages written for these microcomputers assume a full (maximum) memory is present.

What about the new 16-bit microcomputers, and some of the 8-bit ones that allow for more than 64K? Some allow as high as four million bytes. Should you get all the bytes your machine can hold? My answer to this question is partially subjective. Most programs will run in less than 256K of memory, and many in less than 128K. The amount of memory required by the programs you will be using will be the minimum you should consider, of course. Try starting with 96K to 128K of memory, and add more later if you really need it.

Some specialized applications, including the more sophisticated graphics software, and perhaps some large matrix manipulations, might require more memory than 128K. However 128K should be sufficient for most applications and manipulations. Again, get the amount of memory necessary for the programs you will be using. Unless you write your own programs, it doesn't seem likely you will need substantially more than that.

The central component of the computer usually contains the memory, power supply, processing unit, and input/output interfaces for the keyboard, disk drives, terminals, etc. Personal computers are often divided into classes according to whether an 8-bit or a 16-bit microprocessor is used. Some computers have both kinds of microprocessors. The 8- and 16-bits refer to the number of bits on the microprocessor's data bus. (A data bus is an electronic path within a computer that is used to transmit information between the central processing unit and the memory or other input/output devices, called ports.)

Generally, the important difference between 8- and 16-bits is that the 16-bit computer can probably execute mathematical operations more quickly than can an 8-bit system. This is because the 16-bit computer can process larger amounts of information at a time. (However, this is only true if the computer language has been written to take advantage of the 16-bit processor's extra capabilities.) Sixteen-bit computers also usually have a larger addressable memory space. That means a computer with a 16-bit microprocessor can have more memory for programs and data than can an 8-bit system.

Although the 16-bit computer offers some advantages in memory capacity and processing speed, there is a shortage of 16-bit software. Since 8-bit computers have existed longer, most personal computer programs are written for them. So, consider what software you need to do your specific tasks and get the system that has the software you need.

Where to purchase the equipment

Some people prefer to get their system components from several different vendors. The two main reasons for this choice are price and performance. For example, it is often cheaper to buy disk drives and printers from companies other than the one who made the computer. Mail order computer firms are very popular because they are often able to offer lower prices than local stores offering other services for their customers. Sometimes devices from other vendors will outperform the computer manufacturer's counterparts.

The disadvantage of using multiple equipment sources are compatibility and service. Even though Company B says its product will work with that of company A, that is not always the case. Even though the hardware may be compatible, the software may not work. And if the software will not work, it will not make any difference to you if the hardware is compatible or not. For example, my computer and word processing software are from one company, and the printer is from another source. The computer and printer work fine together for ordinary printing tasks. However, the printer cannot properly interpret the underlining and superscripting commands sent to it by the word processing program. If I had purchased a printer from the computer manufacturer, these extra (and very useful) features would be available. As usual, it was a tradeoff between features and price.

When two or more brands of equipment are combined, service can become very difficult to obtain. Some manufacturer's repair facilities will not service other makes of equipment. If company A's disk drive will not work with company B's computer, even though you think they should, each company may place the blame on the other's equipment. And you are stuck with something that will not work. If all of the equipment is from one manufacturer's line, and if the local repair facility has a thorough knowledge of its own equipment, service becomes much easier.

Some areas have system houses, which are places that deal in several lines of equipment and software. The objective of a system house is to provide the system that best fits the customer's needs. System houses provide whatever support is needed for their equipment and programs.

Some companies offer service contracts for their equipment. Service contracts may run from 15% to 25% of the purchase price per year. Microcomputer users are usually responsible for returning the equipment to the nearest service center for repair. When considering what level of service support you need, ask yourself what will happen if the machine cannot be fixed immediately. Can you do without it for two to six weeks? Are loaner machines available? If the machine is crucial to your business, make a contingency plan. If it is important enough, you may have to do something as drastic as purchasing another system for backup protection.

Summary

Do not rush when selecting your computer system. Read whatever information you can find (including documentation manuals), talk to people with similar equipment, discuss your problems with computer sales people, and make a logical decision based upon your best judgment. Do not buy something because it is a particular brand or you like the color of the keyboard. After you buy your system, do not worry too much whether or not you got the best one as long as it does your work satisfactorily.

Chapter 3
Computer networks

Hand-held, programmable calculators have been popular in the last few years with farmers. They have been used to calibrate sprayers, calculate crop yields, figure loan repayment schedules, keep track of machinery costs, and perform many other day-to-day arithmetical operations.

Some state cooperative extension programs have provided listings and instructions for programs in various programmable calculators. Iowa State University in Ames, Iowa, and the Northeast Regional Agricultural Engineering Service at Cornell University in Ithaca, New York, are two of the universities that have provided such a service.

As the need for more complex programs and decision-making aids for the farmer has increased, the capacity of many programmable calculators has been exceeded. Many of the more complex mathematical relationships, such as those needed for computing least-cost feed rations, are too big for the calculators to handle. However, many of the now affordable microcomputing systems have the capacity for these more complicated mathematical formulas and algorithms. With this increased mathematical power comes increased storage. This means easier record-keeping and more detailed analysis of farming enterprise.

But there are still other kinds of information that the farmer or other agriculturalist needs which his personal computer cannot provide.

What about a farmer who needs to know the best times to irrigate? This depends upon his soil type, rainfall, and evapotranspiration. Evapotranspiration is related to the stage of the plant's growth and to the weather. Some of the relationships are very complicated. Information is needed to know when to irrigate based upon the weather and the growth stage of the crop.

When is the best time to market livestock or a crop? What is the grain market today, and how much has it fluctuated in the last three months? What about the other commodity markets?

When is the best time to apply insecticides? In some crops like cotton that require heavy doses of insecticides during the growing season, timing of insecticide applications is critical. Weather affects the reproduction rate of the insects. Stage of plant growth is important. What about insect counts?

Some states have computer programs that have been developed for various personal computers and are available at low cost. Some states can also provide information about programs developed elsewhere. In addition, some of the land grant universities and private firms have developed computer-based communications networks that enable people at remote locations around the state and other states to use a central computer.

As the farmer places a higher monetary value on the timeliness of information, these computer services become more important to him. If he cannot wait for the next newsletter for marketing information, the computer commodity service becomes an important tool in making his management decisions.

Exactly what kind of computer network services are available? In part this is a difficult question to answer because the field is changing so rapidly. One of the best sources of information on services available in your area is the state cooperative extension service. Many states now have a specialist who provides information on the various services available. These specialists are often familiar with the different time-sharing services of interest to the agricultural community.

Two of the more widely-known computer networks used by many different groups of personal computer users are The Source and Compuserve. These two services are available through microcomputer dealers. There are also many "electronic bulletin boards" located around the country, where one can leave notices for other people and can read messages left there by others. The electronic bulletin board provides a way for exchanging information about common problems and interests.

Some commercial services are expanding their services to include as many areas of interest as they believe their customers and potential customers could use. They include such services as electronic banking, major news sources, newspapers and magazines, stock market prices, commodity reports, electronic mail, electronic catalogs for ordering goods, airplane reservations, world wide weather reports, games, and many other features covering a broad range of topics and services. People with common interests have formed users' groups, which are accessed through the computing networks and electronic bulletin boards. These groups can provide a good vehicle for discussing problems of mutual concern with people over a large geographical area.

One of the more recent networks geared toward the agricultural community is AgriStar. According to their literature, "AgriStar is America's agricultural information and computing network." It provides market news, weather reports and forecasts, commodity reports, and many other services.

Equipment Needed

Videotex, or *videotext*, is a relatively recent term used to describe communication between an individual and a remotely-located computer service, usually through the use of a telephone. The user dials the computing service number, places the telephone headset in a device called an "acoustical coupler," which is connected to the terminal or microcomputer, and communicates with the computer using the telephone line.

To communicate with a remote computer, you need (1) a terminal, (2) a modem or acoustical coupler, and (3) a telephone or at least a telephone line.

The terminal

A terminal is an input and output device that sends information to the computer and receives information from it. Information is usually transmitted by typing it on some kind of keyboard. The received information usually appears on a television screen or other display device.

In its simplest form, a terminal does nothing except send and receive messages. It is called a "dumb" terminal. It has no computing power of its own. For many applications, a dumb terminal is all that is needed. If the information received does not need to be analyzed, it is sufficient. However, if the information is to be analyzed or processed, a computer with storage capabilities is required.

Many people use their microcomputer for their remote terminal. With the appropriate computer program and hardware, a computer can behave as if it were simply a terminal for sending and receiving messages. Many can also transmit and receive entire files of information to or from diskettes and cassette tapes. Files of information stored on a cassette or diskette can be analyzed later. A computer program is usually needed for a personal computer to behave as a remote terminal. The dealer from whom the computer was purchased or the place where access to the videotex service was obtained can usually direct you to the appropriate software for your computer.

The modem

Modem is an acronym for a modulator/demodulator. Its function is to change the series of electronic patterns generated by pressing the computer's keys to impulses that can be sent and received through the telephone line. A modem can connect directly between the computer and the phone line. Depending on the type of modem, it may or may not require a telephone to be connected to it. (See Figure 3-1.)

Some modems also have a device that converts the electronic pulses to a series of audible frequency changes which can be sent and received through the handset of a conventional telephone. This device is called an "acoustical coupler" because the computer and the terminal are coupled through the telephone line via a telephone handset.

Acoustical couplers and modems range in price from less than two hundred dollars to several hundred dollars. Most of the ones used with microcomputers operate at one of two rates: 0 to 300 baud, or 1200 baud (see Figures 3-2 and 3-3). As mentioned in chapter 2, the baud rate is a measure of how fast information can be transmitted. Divide the baud rate by 10 to find the maximum number of characters per second that can be

Figure 3-1 • Hayes Plug-in Micromodem II and Terminal Software for Apple II Micro-computer. © 1982, Hayes Microcomputer Products, Inc. (courtesy of Hayes Microcomputer Products, Inc.)

Figure 3-2 • Hayes 300-baud Direct Connect Smartmodem. © 1982, Hayes Microcomputer Products, Inc. (courtesy of Hayes Microcomputer Products, Inc.)

Figure 3-3 • Hayes 1200-baud Direct Connect Smartmodem 1200. © 1982, Hayes Micro-computer Products, Inc. (courtesy of Hayes Microcomputer Products, Inc.)

transmitted. A 300-baud modem allows a maximum transmission of 30 characters per second, and a 1200-baud modem allows a maximum transmission of 120 characters per second.

Generally, the higher baud rate modem is better than the lower rate one. However, several factors must be considered when deciding which rate is best for you. One factor to consider is the transmission rate of the computing service you are using. Many services transmit only at 300 baud. Some transmit at 300 and 1200 baud but charge a higher hourly rate for the higher baud rate.

A second factor is cost. The 1200-baud modems are more expensive than are those in the 0–300 baud range.

A third factor is your own receiving equipment. Some terminals are limited in how fast they can handle received information. The early teletype machines could operate at a maximum of 110 baud. Some of the printing terminals in use today have a maximum speed of 300 baud. If you tried to use one of these terminals with a 1200-baud modem, either nothing would happen or most of the information received would be lost since it would be coming in faster than it could be handled.

A fourth factor to consider is how much information will actually need to be transmitted between the computer and the terminal. If most of the information is sent to the computer from your terminal keyboard, a 300-baud system will be quite sufficient, even for the fast typist. If you are sending or receiving the equivalent of several pages of information on a regular basis, the 1200-baud modem is preferable if the rest of the equipment can utilize it.

The telephone

There are few restrictions on the kind of telephone that will work with a remote computer. However, when you use an acoustic coupler with a telephone, the telephone handset must be the "standard" one. The earpiece and mouthpiece must be on the same unit and shaped to fit into the two rubber cups on the acoustic coupler.

Clear telephone reception is also important. Static on the line could be misinterpreted by your terminal or the central computer as information transmitted from one unit to the other. Be aware of potential problems caused by rainstorms. Remote computer communications would probably be very difficult on a party line. When other people tried to use the line, spurious signals would cause transmission errors between the terminal and the computer. In some cases, these signals could completely disconnect you from the main computer. This has happened in our offices with multiple line telephones when someone picked up the receiver on a line being used for remotely accessing a computer network. Usually the connection was broken completely.

Summary

Should you use a remote computer network? Absolutely. If you need it. You should ask yourself what the time value of the information supplied by the computing service is really worth to your situation. Many of the available services sound very good, and many of them are. But will you use it? If a computing service can supply you with information otherwise unavailable to you or supply it more rapidly than otherwise possible and you need it quickly, then that service is probably worthwhile. Otherwise, it may not be practical to have. Some of the computing services only charge for actual connect time, which is the time you are actually connected to the computer. You may want to try one of these services to determine their real worth to you.

The agricultural community may soon begin to view their computing networks as they do land, machinery, and other resources. The network is another tool that can help them do their job better and more efficiently.

Chapter 4
Programming in BASIC

A computer language allows one to instruct the computer to perform a set of tasks and to furnish it with information or data needed to perform those tasks. The tasks may be adding and subtracting numbers, storing herd records in a disk file, inverting a matrix, printing a letter, drawing a line, calculating the sine of an angle, creating a bar graph on a plotting device, performing a regression analysis, or monitoring the temperature in a grain bin. Every instruction given to a computer must be written in a language that it can understand.

This chapter and the following one explain many of the commands and other language components of the BASIC (BAsic Symbolic Instruction Code) language. BASIC was chosen because some version of it is available on most of the microcomputers available today. The BASIC elements discussed here are primarily, but not exclusively, for Microsoft BASIC. If your particular machine uses some other form of BASIC, you will probaby notice that most of the statements it uses are identical or very similar to the ones discussed here. The greatest variations in the statements will be in the graphics commands and in disk-related operations. Graphics commands are used to instruct the computer to draw lines, circles, triangles, bar charts, and other shapes on a display device. Disk-related operations are commands that determine how information is transferred between a floppy disk or hard disk and the computer's memory.

Before proceeding, let's compare a computer language with other languages. The written form of the English language, like other human languages, contains a set of letters, numbers, and other symbols that can be combined in various ways to express ideas and convey information from one person to another. Certain rules must be followed when these symbols are used for the communication to be successful. For example, periods may only be used at the ends of sentences. A word must always be spelled with the same letters arranged in the same order. Proper names should be capitalized. Text is to be written and read from left to right and from top to bottom.

A computer language is similar to the English language in that it, too, contains a set of letters, numbers, and other symbols, and it has a set of rules governing their use. A major difference between a computer language and a human language is the recipient of the information. Human languages are used by humans to communicate primarily with other humans, whereas computer languages are used by humans to communicate with computers.

Another difference between human and computer languages is that a computer will interpret statements and other language constructs in a consistent, predictable manner. Computer language constructs cannot be interpreted more than one way but interpersonal language can be. When a person reads a letter or story written by another person, the material is interpreted within the framework of the reader's experience, the opinion of the writer, and the reader's perception of the writer's intent.

Because a computer is consistent in its interpretations, the rules of the language must be strictly followed, if man is to successfully communicate with machine. Parentheses, commas, and spaces must always be in their proper places. Words cannot be misspelled. The proper use of symbols and other statements and proper spelling in a computer language is referred to as "syntax." Statements must have the correct syntax for the computer to accept them.

Dialects of a Language

Even when several different microcomputers use the same language, they may have slightly different versions or dialects of the language. This means that while most of the language rules and elements the user learns for one system will be the same for other systems using the same language, there will be some differences.

The different versions of a computer language have an analogy with the English language in the United States. People in Boston and New Orleans both speak English, but it is not exactly the same English although it may be very similar. To communicate with others in different sections of the country, some statements and expressions have to be modified. Some words or phrases will not transfer directly between regions of a country. A "bubbler" in Wisconsin is a "water fountain" in Illinois. A "teeter-totter" in Illinois is a "see-saw" in Louisiana. Similarly, while many of the BASIC statements written for an IBM Personal Computer® can be understood by an Osborne™ or Apple® or Radio Shack® computer, not all of them can be understood.

Evolution of a Language

Computer languages evolve as do human languages, but for different reasons. Human languages evolve as the meaning of words change and as new words are created. Changes in computer languages occur to make the languages easier for people to use and to increase the number and kinds of tasks that the computer can perform with the language. When changes are made in a computer language, the new language is usually referred to as a new "version" or an "update" or as conforming to a certain "standard."

Now we will begin to examine the BASIC language. It is suggested that you study the rest of this chapter and the next chapter with a microcomputer nearby. The concepts and statements can be tested as you read about them. While some things can be learned simply by reading about them, computer programming requires both study and practice.

Constants

Numbers and other data are treated either as constants or variables. A constant is a quantity that has a fixed value. The numbers "2" and "3.141529" are constants. Their values never change. In the equation Y = 7/4, the numbers "7" and "4" are constants. Alphanumeric information, such as people's names or the names of places, are constants.

Constants are often used in computer programs for conversion factors. For example, a program that would change feet to meters would multiply the number of feet by a constant to yield the equivalent number of meters.

Variables

A variable is a quantity whose value can be changed within a computer program. The variable can either have a numeric value or consist of a series of letters, numbers, and other symbols such as an address or telephone number. A variable can have only one value at any one time or place in a program, but this value can change at different times and places within the program. The value of a variable can be changed from one numeric quantity to another or from one set of characters to another. It cannot be changed from a numeric value to a set of characters, or vice versa.

Each variable has a label or name. A variable name is an alphanumeric word that consists of a single letter or a letter followed by one or more alphanumeric characters. (An alphanumeric character is either a letter or a number.) The first character must always be a letter rather than a number or other symbol. For example, valid names in most of the dialects are A, A1, AB, ABC, and R2D2. In some instances, a variable name can have one of the symbols "%," "!," "#," or "$" as the last character. So the variables A%, A1#, AB!, and R2D2$ are also valid in these instances. The meanings of these special symbols will be explained further on in this section. Most BASIC dialects do not allow other non-alphanumeric symbols, including "+," "&," and "@," as valid characters in variable names. Some invalid variable names are 2AB, 3, A$B, AB@, and A%$.

The BASIC interpreter determines the number of characters allowed in a variable name. Some allow a maximum of two characters and others permit six or more. Some versions allow more than two characters, but only the first two are used to identify the variable; the rest of the characters are ignored. That can be confusing if you are not careful. If only the first two characters are used to identify a variable, the variable names STREAM, STEROID, and STRAW are the same variable. Identifying the meaning of the variables is sometimes easier when more than two characters are used. For example, IMPLEMENT is more descriptive than is IM. But you must be cautious to ensure the first two letters of all variables in a program are unique.

Not all computers will support lower case letters. Either the keyboard has no SHIFT key or it does not work with letters. All letters appear as capital letters. For machines that do allow lower case letters, the upper and lower case letters are considered to be the same in variable names. For example, "AB," "Ab," and "ab" would all be the same variable.

Many BASIC dialects allow for four different variable types. They are the integer, single precision, double precision, and string variables. A discussion of each type follows.

(Note: The numerical ranges discussed in the following variable types are typical for 8-bit microcomputing systems, but they may not apply to 16-bit systems. The values given may not be exactly the same as for your computer. Always refer to the owner's manual for the specific details on a particular machine.)

Integer variables

An integer variable contains only integer values. Integers are whole numbers with no fractional parts and no decimal points. The numbers 100, 873, and −200 are integers. Integer variables are designated with a percent sign (%) following the variable name. For example, NA%, R2D2%, and X% are valid integer variable names. The variables AB and AB% are considered by the computer to be separate quantities. AB% is an integer, whereas AB is not. There are upper and lower limits on the size of the allowable integers in BASIC.

On many machines with 8-bit microprocessors, the allowable integer range is from −32768 to 32767. This range is determined by the number of bytes of memory allowed for the variable, and how the computer actually stores the numbers. A byte is the smallest addressable chunk of memory. Two bytes are allocated for each integer variable. Each byte is composed of eight binary digits, or "bits," so each integer uses 16 bits of storage.

Fifteen of the bits represent the magnitude of the variable, and the sixteenth bit indicates its sign. Each bit can have a value of either 0 or 1, which means there are 2 to the 15th power possible combinations of 15 bits. The number 2 raised to the 15th power is 32768, which accounts for the maximum allowable integer value. If a number outside of this range is assigned to an integer variable, either an error occurs and the program stops, or the variable will have a value assigned to it equal to the number modulo 64K.

Modulo refers to the remainder of one number divided by another. The value of 12 modulo 5 is equal to the remainder of 12 divided by 5, or 2. The value of 3 modulo 5 is 3. A number modulo 64K is the remainder of the number when divided by 65,536 (64K).

Single-precision variables

The single-precision variable allows positive and negative numbers with decimal points and fractional components, as well as integer numbers. BASIC usually assumes that a variable name with no special symbol at the end of the variable name is a single-precision variable. Y, Y4, and ABCD are valid single-precision variable names. An exclamation point (!) is sometimes used to designate a single-precision variable. In that case, Y and Y! would be the same variable.

The range of allowable values is determined by the number of bytes allocated to a single-precision variable, often 4 bytes, and by the method used within the machine for storing numbers. (The method for storing numbers containing decimal points and exponents is somewhat complicated, and not really important for most users to understand. It is only important to understand the range and accuracy of the variables, and the amount of memory they require.) The range of a single-precision variable is restricted both in magnitude and in the number of significant digits. A typical range for single-precision variables is $-1*10^38$ to $-1*10^-38$, and $1*10^38$ to $1*10-38$ with seven significant digits. (The symbol " $^$ " means "raised to the power." For example, 4^2 is 4 raised to the power 2, which is 16.) The values 10, 15.45, -2000.9999, and $15.4*10^24$ are valid for single-precision variables. Sometimes a number multiplied by a power of 10 is expressed by the letter "E" followed by the power of 10. The number 1.5E4 is 1.5 multiplied by 10 to the fourth power. So, 1.5E4 is the same as 15000. If the power of 10 is a negative number, it is equivalent to the number divided by the power of 10 raised to that number. Thus, $1.5E-4$ is equal to 0.00015.

Double-precision variables

A double-precision variable has the same magnitude ranges as does the single-precision variable; that is, –1E38 to –1E–38 and 1E38 to 1E–38. However, a double-precision variable has 17 significant digits instead of seven, and occupies eight bytes of storage rather than four. It is designated by the "#" symbol at the end of the variable name. For example, AB#, A#, and R2D2# are double-precision variable names.

String variables

A fourth class of variables is the string variable. A string variable contains a series or a string of letters, numbers, and other symbols, including spaces. The string variable name must end with a dollar sign ($). The variables A$ and NAME$ are string variables. String variables are used to store nonnumeric information. Each character in a string variable requires one byte of storage.

The length of a string variable is usually not defined until it is actually used within a program. String variables are defined by assigning to them a string of characters enclosed in quotation marks ("). For example, R$ = "hello" means R$ would have the word "hello" assigned as its value. The quotation marks are not part of the string. A string variable may be of different lengths at various times in a computer program. It requires one storage location, or byte, for each character in the string, including spaces. For example, consider the string variable NAME$, which contains the string "How now brown cow?." NAME$ would use 18 memory locations—one location for each character including the question mark and one for each space separating the words. If at some later point in the program, NAME$ was redefined by the statement NAME$ = "I am two.", it would then require nine memory locations. The other nine memory locations would be freed for use by other string variables.

Some computers require that a program specify how much memory should be reserved for all of the strings before the rest of the program can be run. The BASIC statement, "CLEAR n," reserves n bytes of memory for string variables in a program. The specification is usually the first or second statement in the program.

Which variable type should you use?

Which variable type to use in a particular situation depends on the number of significant digits needed in the answer and the intermediate calculations and on the storage space available in the computer's memory. For counters (explained later) where the values are often whole numbers and the magnitude of the number does not exceed 32767, an integer variable is adequate. When fractional numbers are required, or the value of the quantity is greater than allowed by an integer quantity, use a single-precision variable. For many financial applications, seven significant digits would not be enough. If seven significant digits are not enough, use a double-precision variable. If 17 digits are inadequate, you may be using the wrong language or the wrong computer, or both.

Another factor to consider when choosing which variable type to use is processing speed. The fewer bytes a variable contains, the faster the computer can process it. Adding two single-precision variables takes less time than does adding two double-precision variables, even when the number stored in both variable types is the same number.

Mathematical Operators

BASIC will perform the operations of addition, subtraction, multiplication, division, and exponentiation. The respective symbols (called "operators"), for these five operations are "+," "−," "*," "/," and "^." The "*" is used for multiplication instead of "X" to enable the computer to differentiate between multiplication and the letter "X" used as part of a variable name. As mentioned earlier, the letter "E" followed by an integer is also a form for expressing numbers raised to a power of 10. For example, 1.5E4 is the same as 15000 and 1.5E−4 is equivalent to 0.00015.

There is a fixed priority for evaluating expressions with more than one operator. Exponentiation has the highest priority, followed by multiplication and division, followed by additions and subtractions. Within each of these three priority groups the operations are performed from left to right within an expression. These priorities can be changed by the programmer with the judicious use of parentheses to force expressions to be evaluated in a desired sequence. The following examples illustrate the priorities used in evaluating the expressions. Assume A=1, B=2, C=3, D=4, and E=5.

```
Y=A+B*C+D      ==> Y=11
Y=A+B*(C+D)    ==> Y=15
Y=(A+B)*(C+D)  ==> Y=21
Y=A+B/C+D/E    ==> Y=2.46667
Y=B^B/C*D/E^B  ==> Y=0.2133
```

Program Statements

A computer program consists of a series of statements. A statement is an instruction or other directive that supplies information to the computer for performing one or more operations. Statements can reserve memory, define functions and variables, supply data, open and close files, begin and end loops, change the value of variables, and send and receive information to other devices such as the screen, keyboard, disk files, printers, and plotters.

One of the most frequently used statements is the assignment statement. In algebra, the equality symbol (=) is used to indicate the quantity on the left side of the symbol is equal to the quantity on the right side of the equation. For example, the equation $X+Y = 16$ means that the sum of the quantities X and Y is equal to 16.

In BASIC, the equal sign (=) does not mean that two quantities are equal. It means to assign the value on the right of the symbol to the variable on the left of the symbol. The value on the left is replaced with the value on the right. The statement $X = Y+4$ says to assign the value of $Y+4$ to the variable X. The left hand side of the statement must always be a single-variable name. For example, the statement $X+Y=16$ is an invalid BASIC assignment statement. It would have to be written either as $X = 16-Y$ or as $Y = 16-X$.

The statement $X = X+1$ is not a valid algebraic equation unless $X = 0$, but it is a valid assignment statement in BASIC. It means to replace the value of X (the left side of the statement) with the value $X+1$ (the right side of the statement). The value of the variable X becomes whatever it was previously, plus one. This kind of statement is used quite often as a counter to record the number of times an event occurs. Every time the statement $X = X+1$ is executed, the value of X is incremented by one. The value could be decremented instead of incremented by using the statement $X = X-1$.

Each line in a BASIC program must have a positive integer line number. Each numbered line can contain one or more BASIC statements. Multiple statements on a line are separated by colons (:). When multiple statements are on a line, all of the statements on that line are processed, in order from left to right, before the next numbered program line is executed. One exception to this is a multiple statement line containing an IF statement. This exception is discussed in the section on the IF/THEN statement. The following is an example of lines with multiple statements:

```
10  CG=15.575:CUBE=123.456
20  A=2:B=3:C=5:
30  D=A+B+C+D:E=CG*CUBE
```

Program lines are executed sequentially from the lowest line number to the highest line number, unless the program flow is interrupted by a special statement to transfer control elsewhere. A program is easier to read and understand if the order of the statements follows the order in which they are executed. For instance, if a program has three sections, one for input, a second for computations, and a third for output, the program statements should start with the input statements followed by the computational statements, and end with the output statements.

An exception is the case where computing time needs to be minimized and an interpreted form of BASIC is used. Then the program statements which are executed most often should be placed closest to the beginning of the program. Most forms of BASIC use an interpreter. An interpreter examines each statement and "interprets" it into a form which the computer can understand. After all of the statements in a program line are executed, the interpreter returns to the beginning of the program and begins searching for the next higher line number. If the lines which are used most often are near the beginning of the program, then less time is used by the interpreter to find them, so the program runs faster. However, unless speed is very important, it is better to write the program statements in the order in which they are executed.

Input and output

A computer program needs a method to communicate with the user and with other devices connected to the computer's processing unit. It usually communicates with the user by printing messages on a screen. It could also use a printer or plotter if these devices were available.

The video screen is an "output device." That is, output, or results, from a computer program is sent to or "output" to it. The user usually sends information to the computer, or "inputs" with the keyboard. Other input devices are the light pen and the track ball. Information sent from the computer's central processing unit is output, and information received by the processing unit is input. Output and input are always determined from the perspective of the computer's central processing unit, not that of the user.

PRINT

To send a message to the screen, BASIC uses the PRINT command. Whatever follows the PRINT command is printed on the screen. If the material following the PRINT command is in quotation marks, it is printed on the screen exactly as it is written within the quotes. The quotation marks themselves are not printed. For example, if

10 PRINT "HELLO, my name is Egor. What is your name?"

was properly executed

HELLO, my name is Egor. What is your name?

would appear on the screen.

If there are no quotes around the information following the PRINT command, the information is considered to be either numbers or variables.

The program

```
10 A=10
20 B=A+20
30 PRINT A,B,45.5
```

would print

```
20   30   45.5
```

on the screen.

```
10 PRINT 10,20,30,40
```

would print

```
10   20   30   40
```

The number of spaces between numbers or messages on a line of output is determined by your particular form of BASIC. Usually numbers separated by commas will be printed at specific tabular settings, just as they are on a typewriter. For example, you might set the tabular spacings on a typewriter at columns 1, 20, 40, 60, etc. After you typed a number, you would tab to the next setting to type the next number. The computer does the same thing with numbers separated by commas. Each new number is printed at the next tabulated setting, which is determined by the computer unless other explicit tab settings are given to it. The user can control how these numbers are printed in most forms of BASIC. The semicolon (;) functions as a tab suppress. When it is used in place of a comma to separate numbers, variables, or text in a PRINT statement, the information is printed with no spaces between the items and no tabs. If there is no semicolon at the end of a PRINT statement, the next PRINT output begins on the following line. A semicolon at the end of a PRINT statement will cause the next PRINT statement to continue on the same line as the last one. The word PRINT with no text following it causes a blank line to be printed. For example,

```
10 PRINT "THIS IS PART OF LINE ONE";
20 PRINT "AND THIS IS THE REST OF IT."
30 PRINT
40 PRINT "HELLO. ISN'T IT A NICE DAY?"
50 END
```

would print the message

THIS IS PART OF LINE ONE AND THIS IS THE REST OF IT.

HELLO. ISN'T IT A NICE DAY?

TAB

The tab positions can be controlled with the TAB(n) function, where n is the column number for the tab. Unlike a typewriter, the TAB function only works for the immediate statement using it. It does not change the default settings of BASIC. (A default setting is an assumption which the computer makes. It will use the default setting unless explicitly directed otherwise. For example, the computer's tabulated settings might have default values of every 10 spaces. That means the first number would start in column 1, the second in column 10, the third in column 20, etc.) To print the variables A, B, and C beginning in columns 15, 40, and 60, use the statement

PRINT TAB(15);A;TAB(40);B;TAB(60);C

SPC

The space function, SPC(n), is similar to the TAB function except that it moves the cursor n spaces to the right of the present cursor position instead of n spaces from the left margin. If the TAB in the last PRINT statement was replaced with the SPC function, we would have the following:

PRINT SPC(15);A;SPC(40);B;SPC(60);C

In this case the variable A would still be printed beginning in column 15, since the first space function moved the cursor 15 columns to the right of the left margin. The SPC(40) function moved the cursor 40 spaces to the right of the last printed digit of variable A. The third SPC caused C to be printed 60 columns to the right of B. SPC is often used in a single line of output to ensure there are a sufficient number of spaces between variables and/or text. But, the TAB should be used when printing columnar data, because TAB makes it easier to align columns than does SPC, particularly when the numbers have varying numbers of digits.

Printing on a line printer is done in the same manner as on the computer's display screen except that LPRINT or LPRINT USING is used instead of PRINT and PRINT USING. (The PRINT USING statement Is discussed in the next chapter.) Some interpreters do not use the LPRINT. They consider the screen as one of many output devices, along with a line printer or plotter and disk drives. The program informs the computer which device is to be used for the output, so the form of the PRINT statement is the same for all output devices. This method is system dependent, so you must once again refer to your system's instructions for details.

INPUT

A computer will often need information from the user while a program is running. For example, a program that converts temperatures from Fahrenheit to Centigrade would need to know what temperature to convert. The user may have to choose from a set of options at certain places in the program. A user may want the computer to print the results, or draw a bar chart, for instance. The user has to be able to enter data into a program during execution. One way of accomplishing this is with the INPUT statement. It has the form INPUT A, where A is a variable name. The variable A could be an integer, a single-precision, a double-precision, or a string variable. When the INPUT statement is reached during the execution of a program, the computer stops, prints a blinking question mark on the screen, and waits for the user to enter the appropriate value by typing keys on the keyboard.

After the value is entered and the RETURN or ENTER key is pressed, the variable in the INPUT statement is assigned whatever value was entered, and the program continues with the next statement. The INPUT statement will usually allow an alphanumeric string to be inserted before the variable name to serve as an explanation or "prompt" for the user. For example:

```
10 INPUT "ENTER YOUR NAME ";NAME$
20 INPUT "ENTER YOUR AGE ";AGE
30 PRINT
40 PRINT "HELLO, ";NAME$
50 PRINT "YOU ARE ";AGE;" YEARS OLD. I AM GLAD TO MEET
   YOU."
60 END
```

This program would cause the following exchange to take place. The name Henrietta and the number 21 would be entered by the program user, and the RETURN or ENTER key would be pressed after each entry:

```
ENTER YOUR NAME HENRIETTA
ENTER YOUR AGE 21

HELLO, HENRIETTA
YOU ARE 21 YEARS OLD. I AM GLAD TO MEET YOU.
```

If a statement of the form INPUT B was used with no statement in quotations preceding the variable B, the computer would display a blinking "?" with no explanation and wait for a response from the user before continuing.

READ and DATA

Another way of entering data into a program is with a combination of READ and DATA statements. A READ statement gets information from a DATA statement located somewhere in the program instead of from the keyboard. It has the form READ A, where A is again a variable name. Multiple values could be read in at one time with a statement like READ A1,A2,A3. When the READ statement is encountered, the computer searches for a DATA statement and reads as many values as there are variables in the READ statement. Let's try some examples.

Example 1

```
10 READ A,B,C
20 PRINT A+B,C
25 DATA 1,2,17.5
30 END
```

prints

3   17.5

Example 2

```
10 READ A,B,C$,D$,E,F
20 DATA 4,5,"MARY, MARY "
30 DATA "QUITE CONTRARY",19,384
40 PRINT C$;D$
50 PRINT "A+B = ";A+B
60 PRINT E,F,E−F
70 END
```

prints

MARY, MARY QUITE CONTRARY
A+B = 9
19   19.384   18.616

DATA statements can be located anywhere in a program, including before the READ statement. Two logical places for DATA statements are either immediately following their corresponding READ statements or in one area of the program where all of the DATA statements are grouped together. Whenever a READ is encountered, the program always goes to the first DATA statement in the program, and then to consecutive ones until it gets all of the required data or runs out of values. If the computer tries to read and there is no data, an error will occur, and the program will stop.

A program command sometimes used in conjunction with the READ and DATA statements is the RESTORE command. RESTORE causes the next READ statement to begin reading data from the first item in the first DATA statement in the program. This command is useful if the same data needs to be used more than once.

IF/THEN (ELSE)

Many times a program needs to perform different operations, depending upon the result of some operation. The decision whether or not to do a particular task depends upon whether a condition is true or false. A statement that can accomplish this function is the IF/THEN statement. It can have different forms:

```
10 IF A = B THEN 200
20 IF A > B THEN C = 25
30 IF A < B−20 THEN D = D−1
40 IF A <= B−25 THEN D = D−2
```

These four examples show some of the forms this construct can take. Line 10 says to check if the variables A and B have the same value (are equal). If the two values are equal, the program jumps to line 200; otherwise it continues to the next program step. Line 20 says that if the variable A is greater than B, then set the variable C equal to 25. Line 30 compares A with the value B−20. If A is less than B−20, one is subtracted from the value of the variable D. Line 40 determines if A is less than or equal to B−25. If this condition is true, the value of D is reduced by two. Any variables that are compared with constants or other variables in the IF statement are unchanged after the test. The values of variables A and B are unaffected in lines 10 through 40 of this example.

Another form of the IF/THEN statement is the IF/THEN ELSE command. This second form performs one task if the expression following the IF is true, otherwise (ELSE) it performs the second task. For example:

```
50 IF CLOUD<>DARK THEN TEMP=HOT ELSE TEMP=COOL
```

Line 50 checks for the condition of the variable CLOUD being unequal to the variable DARK. If CLOUD is unequal to DARK, TEMP is set equal to

HOT. Otherwise, CLOUD is equal to DARK, and TEMP is set equal to COOL.

Another example is:

60 IF Q$="YES" THEN 200 ELSE 400

This statement sends the program to line 200 if Q$ is YES, and to line 400 otherwise. Line 60 brings up an important point: Q$ must be EXACTLY equal to YES for the program to go to line 200. If Q$ was Yes, or yes, or YES followed by a space, control would go to line 400.

Now, let's look at a simple program that incorporates some IF/THEN statements. It is a program that converts inches to meters, which might need to be run several times if the user has several conversions he or she wishes to make. The programmer can handle this situation by having the program ask the user whether to continue or quit after each conversion. The program would continue or stop, depending upon the response to the question. Our program will ask for a number in inches, convert it to meters, print the answer, and then ask if there are more numbers to convert. If there are more numbers, the program will start again. If not, it will stop.

```
10 PRINT "INCHES TO METERS CONVERSION PROGRAM"
20 INPUT "ENTER VALUE TO CONVERT, IN INCHES ";I
30 M=I*2.54/100
40 PRINT I;" INCHES IS EQUAL TO ";M;" METERS"
50 INPUT "ENTER Q TO QUIT OR ANY OTHER KEY TO CONTINUE ";Q$
60 IF Q$<>"Q" THEN 20 ELSE END
```

This program will stop when the operator enters a Q in response to the question in line 50. If any other letter is entered, the program will go to line 20, ask for a new value, and repeat the process.

An IF/THEN command can cause problems when used in a multiple statement line. Consider this example:

```
100 INPUT "ENTER C TO CONTINUE OR Q TO QUIT ";A$
110 IF A$="Q" THEN 300:I=I+1:Y=2*I
120 B=B+23
                              . . .
300 END
```

The user is prompted whether to continue or quit in line 100. If Q is entered, the program goes to line 300 and stops. If the user responds with a C or any other character, the result of the IF test in line 100 is false, and the program continues with line 120. The other two statements in line 110 will never be executed. It is usually a good idea not to have any statements in a program line following an IF/THEN statement.

Another potential problem with IF tests is when single-precision or double-precision numbers are tested for equality either with other single- or double-precision numbers or with constants. Because of the way fractional values are stored in the computer's memory, two numbers may be very close to each other but still not be exactly the same. For instance, if 0.1 was added 10 times to 1.0, the result might not be exactly 2.0. It might be 1.99999999. When using single- or double-precision variables in comparison tests, it is much better to test for inequalities. Following is a good and a poor example of an IF test:

Use

```
10 IF A<B THEN 100
20 IF A <= B THEN 200
30 IF A > 1.9 THEN 300
40 IF A# >= 10.173458 THEN 400
```

Do not use

```
10 IF A = B THEN 100
20 IF A = 1.999 THEN 200
30 IF A <> B THEN 300
40 IF A# = 19.163458 THEN 400
```

The array

An array is a set or list of numbers or other related information. An array of names might be a list of names that the programmer wished to group together (for example, cow identification numbers in a dairy herd). BASIC uses a dimension statement, DIM, to define an array size. The statement DIM NAME(50) defines a variable array, NAME, with 50 elements. The first element in the array is referenced by NAME(1), the second element by NAME(2), etc. The numbers in the parentheses are called "subscripts" or "indexes" to the array elements. Some forms of BASIC begin an array with element number zero, in which case our dimension statement would reserve room for 51 numbers and the first element would be NAME(0). But for our discussion, we will assume the first element is number 1, so the example would reserve space for 50 elements.

An array can have multiple dimensions. Its dimension is determined by the number of subscripts in the DIM statement. DIM N(50) creates a one-dimensional array with 50 elements. DIM N(50,2) defines a two-dimensional array with 100 elements. The number of array elements is equal to the product of all of the subscripts in the DIM statement. A statement of the form DIM N$(50,2) would provide for 50×2, or 100 strings. N$(10,1) might represent the name of the 10th person in the list, and N$(10,2) could contain the telephone number of that same person. Multiple-dimensioned arrays are used to store sets of related information, such as matrices, mailing lists with names and addresses, parts descriptions and order numbers, etc. The number of dimensions allowed in an array is determined by your particular BASIC interpreter and the amount of memory available for holding the array.

All array dimensions must be the same type. One array could not contain both integers and double-precision numbers. The variable type of an array is defined the same way as undimensioned variables. Usually the same variable name cannot be used in a program both as a dimensioned and as an undimensioned variable. For example, the following program

```
10 DIM N(50)
20 N = 15
30 N(2) = 10
```

would cause an execution error when line 20 was reached because an attempt was made to use N both as a single variable name and as an array.

Elements in an array are defined the same way as are undimensioned variables. For example:

```
10 NAME(1)=100.5
20 NA$(2)="MARY HAD A LITTLE LAMB"
30 NA#(5)=1234567890
```

FOR/NEXT (STEP)

A "loop" is a term used to describe a set of instructions that can be executed several times. The instructions are "looped" through from the first to the last as many times as needed. The first statement in a loop is in the form

```
FOR A = B TO C STEP D
```

where A is a numerical variable, and B, C, and D are either numerical variables or constants.

The FOR statement tells the computer to loop through the following instructions a certain number of times. The number of times the loop is performed is determined by the values of B, C, and D. The first time through the loop, variable A has a value equal to B. Execution of the statements following the FOR statement continue in order until a NEXT A statement is encountered. A is then incremented by an amount equal to D, which is the "step" or incremental value.

The STEP can be a fractional or integer value. If STEP D is omitted from the FOR statement, an increment of one is assumed. If the newly incremented value of A is less than or equal to the value of C, the computer returns to the first statement following the FOR statement. This process continues until the value of A exceeds that of C. Then the program continues with the statement following NEXT A. Here are some ways of using a FOR/NEXT loop:

Program #1

```
10 FOR I=2 TO 5 STEP 0.5
30 J=2*I
40 PRINT I,J
50 NEXT I
60 END
```

Output

```
2      4
2.5    5
3      6
3.5    7
4      8
4.5    9
5      10
```

The increment for a FOR/NEXT loop defaults to 1 if the STEP is omitted:

Program #2

```
10 A=2
20 B=5
30 FOR I=A TO B
40 J=2*I+4
50 PRINT A,B,I,J
60 NEXT I
70 END
```

Output

```
2    5    2    8
2    5    3    10
2    5    4    12
2    5    5    14
```

FOR/NEXT loops will allow negative values, and STEP can be greater than 1:

Program #3

```
10 A=−2
20 B=3
30 C=2
40 FOR I=A TO B STEP C
50 PRINT I
60 NEXT I
70 END
```

Output

```
−2
0
2
```

You can also use decrementing loops by using a negative value for the STEP:

Program #4

```
10 A=8
20 B=4
30 C=−1
40 FOR I=A TO B STEP C
50 PRINT I
60 NEXT I
70 END
```

Output

```
8
7
6
5
4
```

Subroutines

A subroutine is a section of a program that is used many times. Instead of rewriting it each place in the program that it is needed, the subroutine is written once and "called" whenever it is needed. The last statement in a subroutine is always a RETURN statement. RETURN tells the computer to return to the place in the program that called the subroutine. Subroutines can be called with either the GOSUB or the ON X GOSUB statement.

GOSUB 100 calls a subroutine that begins at line 100. The program continues from line 100 until a RETURN statement is reached. The RE-

TURN statement causes the program to return to the next statement following the GOSUB 100. A subroutine call can be made from anywhere in the program to anywhere else in the program, except from within the subroutine itself.

ON X GOSUB 100,200,300 is a conditional form of the subroutine call. The subroutine called is dependent upon the value of X. The symbol X is allowed to have positive integer values. If X = 1, subroutine 100 is called. If X = 2, subroutine 200 is called, etc. In this example, an error would occur if X had a value other than 1, 2, or 3. However, the number of subroutines that can be called with this form of calling statement is not limited to three. It can be any arbitrary number depending upon the limitations of the particular BASIC used.

Here is an example of where a subroutine might be used. Consider a program that needed to have several dates input from the keyboard. The month, day, and year were to be entered separately. This input could be accomplished either by writing three statements every time the date was needed or by writing a date subroutine. For example:

```
10 INPUT "ENTER MONTH ";D1$
20 INPUT "ENTER DAY ";D2$
30 INPUT "ENTER YEAR ";D3$
```

If these three statements were written every time a date was needed, the program would work fine. But, writing the statements each time requires more space in the computer's memory, in addition to the extra effort of rewriting the same code several times. If, however, the date section was written as a subroutine, the three lines just mentioned, followed with a RETURN statement, need be written only once. Whenever a date was needed, the subroutine would be called by a GOSUB 10 statement.

Suppose a program was written that needed the date in lines 200, 250, and 310. This could be done as follows:

```
5 GOTO 50
10 INPUT "ENTER MONTH ";D1$
20 INPUT "ENTER DAY ";D2$
30 INPUT "ENTER YEAR ";D3$
40 RETURN
50 REM the next program statement would begin here
       . . .
200 GOSUB 10
       . . .
250 GOSUB 10
       . . .
310 GOSUB 10
       . . .
500 END
```

Summary

When you have finished reading this chapter, you should have enough information to write some programs. I suggest you try writing some simple programs before proceeding to the next chapter. You probably will not even need a flowchart for them. Flowcharts are usually unnecessary for programs with fewer than 50 lines. Programming is best mastered by learning a few statements, using them, then learning a few more statements and using them. Most people will forget what they have read if too many commands are studied before any of them are used.

Chapter 5
Advanced topics in BASIC

This chapter deals with some of the more advanced features of the BASIC language. These features allow more sophisticated and complex programming. They may not be necessary for many programs, particularly those whose primary function is the immediate calculation of a set of input values. That is, if information does not need to be stored in a file or to be sorted or classified, these features may not be needed. There is no particular significance to the order in which the following concepts are discussed. All of the commands and procedures are useful in particular situations.

SWAP

SWAP A,B is used to exchange the values of variables A and B, where A and B are any two variable names. They can be numerical or string variables. For example:

```
10 X=2
20 Y=5
30 PRINT X,Y
40 SWAP X,Y
50 PRINT X,Y
60 END
```

Line 30 prints the values 2 and 5 for variables X and Y, respectively. Line 40 exchanges the values of X and Y, so line 50 prints the values 5 and 2 to be printed for X and Y.

Swapping is particularly useful for sorting lists in descending or ascending order. Suppose a dimensioned array, A, had 50 elements that were already defined when the following section of code is encountered. (Code is one or more program statements.) This program will rearrange the values of the array in order from the smallest value to the largest. The smallest value will be in cell A(1) and the largest will be in A(50).

```
900 REM SORT AN ARRAY IN ASCENDING ORDER
1000 FOR X=1 TO 49
1010 I=0
1020 FOR Y=1 TO 49
1030 IF A(Y+1)<A(Y) THEN SWAP A(Y),A(Y+1):I=1
1040 NEXT Y
1050 IF I=0 THEN 1070
1060 NEXT X
1070 END
```

The program uses X and Y as counters. As Y goes from 1 to 49, the value of each array element is compared with the next higher numbered element. If the lower numbered element has a greater value than the next element, the two values are exchanged and the variable I has its value changed from 0 to 1. This proceeds until each element is compared to the one following it. At this point the program is at line 1050. Variable I is compared with zero. If it is equal to zero, that means no exchanges have occurred between any two cells. This could only happen if each cell has a value no greater than the one following it. That is, the array is now sorted in ascending order and the program stops. If I is not equal to zero, at least one exchange has been made and the comparison of each pair of adjoining cells begins anew. After a maximum of N−1 sets of comparing all adjoining cells, where N is the number of elements in the array, the array is sorted. The program would have worked just as well without using the variable I. The purpose of variable I is to reduce the number of times that a set of comparisons has to be made if the array is completely sorted before N−1 sets have been compared.

This sorting technique is sometimes called "bubble sorting." It is not particularly efficient for very large arrays, but it is simple and it works. It can be used for functions such as alphabetizing lists of names. What if array A was changed to array A$ (an array of string variables), and each element of A$ contained a name with the last name first and the first name last? The bubble sorting program would alphabetize the names with the "Allens" at the beginning of the array and the "Zimbrowskis" at the end. However, this technique would not work if the names were listed as first names followed by last names.

If a particular version of BASIC does not have the SWAP A,B command, it can be emulated by using

```
10 TEMP=A:A=B:B=TEMP
```

instead of

```
10 SWAP A,B
```

Programming Errors

Programming errors can be either syntax or logical errors. A syntax error occurs when a BASIC statement is misspelled or a statement is written in a form unacceptable to the interpreter or compiler. For example:

```
10 Y=%A+2
20 X+Y=2
```

Line 10 contains a syntax error because a variable name cannot start with the percent symbol (%). Line 20 produces a syntax error since arith-

metic operations are not allowed on the left hand side of an equal symbol
(=).

A logical error is caused when the program produces an invalid
result or tries to perform an illegal operation, even though the syntax is
correct. For example:

```
100  A=0
110  B=10
120  Y=B/A

              . . .

800  DIM Q(15)
810  Q(16)=27
```

Statements 100, 110, and 120 all have correct syntax. But line 120 will
produce a logical error when it is executed because a division by zero is
undefined. Line 810 causes a logical error in execution because an attempt is made to define an array element outside the defined array size.
Logical errors frequently occur when variables take on unexpected or
unknown values. For instance, more likely an error would have been
encountered in line 810 when it had the form

```
140  Q(X)=27
```

and X assumed a negative value or a value greater than 15 sometime
earlier in the program.

Logical errors also occur when a program does not follow the expected sequence of events. This change of sequence occurs when program control is transferred to the wrong statement by a GO TO or an IF
statement. These errors may be difficult to detect unless the user knows
the exact sequence of steps followed by the computer. The TRACE function is useful in determining this sequence.

TRACE

The TRACE feature instructs the computer to print each statement number on the screen as that statement is executed. It produces a "trace" of
the path the program follows during execution. Tracing is very useful for
debugging a program. As previously mentioned, "debugging" means
correcting the logical errors in a program. When the TRACE feature is
activated, it becomes obvious which program statements are executed
and at what times they are executed. The TRACE function can be turned
on and off whenever desired. To turn on the TRACE, type "TRON." Type
"TROFF" to turn it off. In complicated programs, the TRACE may be
turned on and off several times during the program to examine the program in selected areas.

VAL(X$)

The VAL(X$) command returns the numerical value of the string variable X$. It terminates with the first character in the string that has no meaning in a numerical value. For example, if X$ = "700 dollars," the statement PRINT VAL(X$) would print the number "700" (without quotation marks). VAL only considers numbers, decimal points, and the letter "E" (for exponent) as valid characters. A COMMA IS NOT A VALID NUMERICAL CHARACTER. The VAL function will stop when it encounters a comma in a string. Consider this program and its output:

```
10  X$="123,456.25"
20  PRINT VAL(X$)
30  X$="123456.25"
40  PRINT VAL(X$)
50  END
```

The output would be as follows:

```
123
123456.25
```

BASIC considers commas as separators between numbers or other pieces of data, just as it considers blank spaces as separators.

The VAL function is useful in getting numerical value from disk files when the information has been stored on the disk in string form. It is not unusual to store numeric information in string form, particularly in random access files. VAL is also useful for checking for valid data entries from the keyboard. Suppose a program needed the price of wheat in dollars and cents per bushel. If the price per bushel variable was called "PRICE," the simplest way to accept the keyboard entry would be with a statement such as

```
10  INPUT "ENTER PRICE OF WHEAT - PER BUSHEL BASIS ";PRICE
```

If the user entered $7.25, the program would either stop because of an error in input (it expected a number and got a nonnumerical value) or print a cryptic message such as "REDO FROM START." If the price was $1,000 per bushel and 1,000 was entered, a statement such as "EXTRA IGNORED" might appear and the program would continue. In either situation, the user may be confused by the computer's response. The VAL function provides a better way of getting the information. For example:

```
10  INPUT "ENTER PRICE OF WHEAT - PER BUSHEL BASIS ";Q$
20  PRINT "IS ";VAL(Q$);" THE CORRECT VALUE":INPUT A$
30  IF A$="Y" THEN PRICE=VAL(Q$) ELSE GOTO 10
```

Instead of using PRICE as the input variable, the information is entered as a string. The value of the string is printed, and the user is queried if that value is correct. If it is correct, PRICE is set equal to that value and the program continues. If it is not correct, the user is allowed to reenter the value. Invalid entries would be immediately obvious. The value of $7.25, for example, would be zero. The value of 1,000 would be one. You may be thinking that the desired format should have been explained in the question and I would agree with you. The question could be clarified by using

```
10 INPUT "ENTER PRICE OF WHEAT - PER BUSHEL WITH NO DOLLAR
   SIGNS OR COMMAS ";Q$
```

Even with this clarification, the program should probably be written to allow the user to check for errors.

INKEY$

The INKEY$ command checks the keyboard input buffer to determine if any key has been pressed since the last INPUT, LINEINPUT, or INKEY$ statement. If no key has been pressed, INKEY$ is equal to a null character or empty string (""). If a key has been pressed, INKEY$ contains the ASCII code for the key pressed most recently. It does not echo the character to the screen as do the INPUT and LINEINPUT statements. (Echoing a character means that whatever key is pressed is also printed on the screen.)

INKEY$ is useful when the response to a question can be made by pressing only one key. It does not require the ENTER or RETURN key to be pressed, as do other forms of input statements. If a menu (a list of programs or functions from which the user may choose) is printed, a letter or number may be listed for each choice, and the user need only press the key corresponding to his or her choice.

The INKEY$ function is also useful if the computer is performing many calculations, and the user needs to temporarily stop the program or transfer control to some other portion of the program. For instance, if a large amount of information is being printed, the user may want to stop after a partial listing if the information is invalid or if he needs to change something. One way the user can stop the program is with a BREAK key, which stops the program completely. The disadvantage of using the BREAK key is that all of the information has to be reentered to rerun the program. If the program itself checked occasionally to see if the user wanted to stop, it could stop itself and still retain all of its data. The user can do this using a subroutine call. Suppose the user wants to check after every 50 lines of output to see if the program should stop but does not want the program to wait for a response to continue. He or she could accomplish this faster by inserting a GOSUB 1000 subroutine after each 50 lines of printed output, along with the following code:

```
1000 Q$=INKEY$
1010 IF Q$="" THEN RETURN
1020 '    ENTER STATEMENTS HERE TO REACT TO WHATEVER KEY
1030 '    HAS BEEN PRESSED
```

Whenever the subroutine is called, the keyboard buffer is interrogated. If a key has not been pressed, the program returns to where it was and continues without interruption. If a key has been pressed, Q$ will not be equal to a null string. Statements would be entered here to transfer control to different parts of the program, dependent upon which key had been pressed.

DEF FNA

DEF FNA(b,c,d)=formula is a statement that defines a function to be used at other points in a program. A function is a single statement subroutine that does not require a RETURN statement and can be called from anywhere in the program after it has once been defined. The function name (A in this example) can be any legal variable name. It can be a single-precision, double-precision, or string variable function. The number of arguments (b, c, and d in this example) can vary from none up to a large number, depending upon your particular BASIC interpreter. The formula is any valid expression. Functions are useful in programs that need to perform a particular set of operations on a set of variables. Following are some examples.

Consider a program that calculates the hypotenuse of several different right triangles. The hypotenuse of a right triangle is equal to the square root of the sum of the squares of the two other sides. It is expressed as the following equation in BASIC

```
420 HYP=SQR(A*A+B*B)
```

where SQR is a built-in BASIC function for calculating the square root of a nonnegative numerical expression. One way to calculate the hypotenuse would be to write a form of this equation everywhere in the program that it is needed. A second, more efficient way would be to define a function HYP, which would calculate the hypotenuse for us and would only have to be inserted into the code one time:

```
20 DEF FNHYP(A,B)=SQR(A*A+B*B)
```

Now, whenever the hypotenuse of a right triangle with sides X and Y is needed in the program, the user need only insert the statement HYP(X,Y) wherever the hypotenuse is desired. In the DEF FN statement the variables A and B, called "arguments," are replaced by whatever variables are used whenever the HYP function is needed. When using the defined function, be certain to use the same number of arguments as there were when the function was originally defined. The user can place the DEF FN function statement anywhere in a program, but he or she should probably place it near the beginning. This is because it cannot be used by any statements that precede it since it would not yet have been defined (assuming the statements were executed in order).

Another example is a program that requires several dates be entered in the form of the MM/DD/YYYY, where MM is the month, DD is the day of the month, and YYYY is the year. The date must be entered in this format since the program assumes the information always be entered as such. A function statement can be used to test the validity of the format. The date will be considered valid if MM is greater than 0 and less than 13. DD can range from 1 to 31, and YYYY will be arbitrarily restricted to values greater than 1950 for the sake of our example. The function will be TRUE if the date is valid and FALSE if it is invalid. (There is no reason to check the "/" symbols, so they will be ignored. That is, the date could be entered as MM#DD#YYYY and still be valid.) The program would be as follows:

```
10 DEF FNOK(D$)=(O<VAL(LEFT$(D$,2))) AND
(VAL(LEFT$(D$,2))<13))) AND (0<VAL(MID$(D$,4,2))) AND
(VAL(MID$(D$,4,2)<32)) AND (1950<VAL(MID$(D$,6,4)))
```

The function may look a little complicated. It includes both string operators and logical operators. It consists of five logical tests separated by AND operators. Remember that AND means a statement is TRUE if both A and B are TRUE, where A and B are the expressions to the left and right of the AND. The first test is valid if the value of the month, MM, which is the two characters at the far left of the string D$, is greater than 0. The next test on these same two characters is valid if their value is less than 13. The third and fourth tests use the MID$ function to extract the substring, which consists of the fourth and fifth characters of the string D$. The value of this substring must be greater than zero and less than 32. The final test examines the value of characters 7 through 11 in the string D$ to ensure that it is greater than 1950. If all five of these tests are TRUE, then OK is set to TRUE; otherwise it returns a FALSE value.

A statement such as one of the following can be used whenever the validity of a date is in question:

```
1010 INPUT" ENTER DATE (MM/DD/YYYY) ";A$
1020 IF NOT(OK(A$)) THEN 1010
```

Statement 1020 says if the date is not correct, the user should ask for the date to be reentered. In this example, the year was restricted to values greater than 1950. If the year was restricted to different ranges at different points in the program, the function could be redefined using arguments that would represent the upper and lower bounds for the year.

```
10 DEF FNOK(D$,LOWER,UPPER)=(O<VAL(LEFT$(D$,2))) AND
(VAL(LEFT$(D$,2))<13))) AND (0<VAL(MID$(D$,4,2))) AND
(VAL(MID$(D$,4,2)<32)) AND (LOWER<VAL(MID$(Q$,7,4))) AND
(VAL(MID$(Q$,7,4))<UPPER)
```

In this case, the function would be called by

```
1020 IF NOT(OK(A$,1950,1980) THEN 1010
```

where 1950 and 1980 represent the lower and upper bounds in a particular situation.

RND(X)

The RND(X) function returns a value between 1 and X. If X=0, a value between 0 and 1 is generated. RND(X) is a pseudo-random number generator. That means it generates a fixed, repeatable set of numbers which are uniformly distributed over a selected range of numbers. Most versions of BASIC have some kind of random number generator. Some only generate values between 0 and 1. Numbers outside that range can be derived with a little additional effort on the part of the programmer. For example, to generate random number values for a variable Y in the interval from 0 to 100, use Y = 100*RND(X) instead of Y = RND(X). To generate random numbers in a range which excludes 0, use statements like the following:

```
10 '    RANDOM NUMBER GENERATOR FOR NUMBERS FROM 5 TO 10
20 Y=10*RND(X)
30 IF Y<5 THEN 20
```

This program would only proceed past line number 30 when a random number in the range from 5 and 10 was generated.

Other random number generators can also generate random integer numbers for any range of 1 to X, as long as X does not exceed the generator's upper limit. Consult your computer's reference book to determine the specifics of your random number generator.

A random number generator is particularly useful in simulating stochastic processes. A stochastic process is a process with more than one possible outcome, with each outcome occurring with a certain probability. Rolling a die is an example of a stochastic process. The probability of getting a six on any given roll is 1/6. Reaching a traffic intersection while the traffic signal is red is another example. Assuming each traffic signal is independent of all other traffic signals, the probability of the light being red at the moment you reach it equal to the total time the light is red in one complete cycle divided by the total cycle time.

Rainfall might be considered a stochastic process if one considers an entire growing season. Suppose a user wanted a computer program that would determine the days available for field work during a growing season. The days available for field work will be dependent upon the amount of rainfall. Let us assume that a farmer can work all day in the field if it does not rain that day. We will assume the farmer can work one-half of a day if it rains less than 0.1 inch, but cannot work at all if it rains more than 0.1 inch. Further let us assume that, based upon weather records and field records, the probability of it not raining on any given day is 0.8, the probability of it raining less than 0.1 inches is 0.15, and the probability of it raining more than 0.1 inches is 0.05. The question is to find how many days we can expect to be able to work in the field during a particularly 120 day period. The following program could do this:

```
10 DAYS=0
20 FOR X=1 TO 120
30 Y=RND(0)
40 IF Y<=0.8 THEN DAYS=DAYS+1:NEXT X
50 IF Y<=0.95 THEN DAYS=DAYS+0.5
60 NEXT X
70 PRINT "THERE ARE ";DAYS;" DAYS AVAILABLE FOR FIELD WORK"
80 END
```

DAYS will be our counter for the number of days of field work. Y will be assigned a uniformly distributed value between 0 and 1 in line 30. Line 40 tests for a no-rain condition. That is, if Y is less than or equal to 0.8, which is the probability of no rain occurring on any given day, we assume it did not rain. In that case, a full day is worked, and the FOR/NEXT loop increments its counter and returns to line 30 and continues. If Y is greater than 0.8, line 50 tests if it is less than or equal to 0.95. Y will have a value between 0.8 and 0.95 with a probability of 0.15, which is the probability of it raining less than 0.1 inch. If this is true, one-half day is spent in the field, and the FOR/NEXT loop counter increments and continues. If Y is greater than 0.95, it rained more than 0.1 inch, and no field work is performed, so the simulation goes to the next day.

One other very important assumption was made in this simulation. Field work on any day was assumed to be independent of the previous weather. If it rained 12 inches yesterday but did not rain today, the program assumes field work can be done today. In reality this is not true, of

course, and a more realistic program would have to take into consideration the previous rainfall.

LINE INPUT A$

A LINE INPUT statement is used to accept data in a manner similar to an
INPUT statement. One difference is the INPUT accepts information up to,
but not including, a comma, or until the RETURN or ENTER (or the ASCII
Line Feed or Carriage Return characters are encountered) keys are
pressed. The LINE INPUT accepts information until the RETURN or ENTER
key is pressed. This function is important when the data is a name such as
"Smith, Powers A." or "Robert Metcalf, III" or a town and state like
"Arthur, Illinois." If an INPUT statement was used to accept this data
from the keyboard, only part of it would be taken.

Suppose the two names and addresses were input using the statements INPUT N1$, INPUT N2$, and INPUT ADR$ (each as a separate
BASIC statement). If N1$, N2$ and ADR$ were then printed, the results
would be

        Smith
        Robert Metcalf
        Arthur

Everything to the right of the comma would be ignored, and the message
"EXTRA IGNORED" would be printed on the screen. This message means
the computer knew there was a comma and probably some more information after it, but it ignored whatever it was. If, however, the statements
LINE INPUT N1$, LINE INPUT N2$, and LINE INPUT ADR$ were used, and
the three variables were printed, the result would be

        Smith, Powers A.
        Robert Metcalf, III
        Arthur, Illinois

LINE INPUT is only used with string variables and not with numerical
variables. If commas will never be used in the input strings, there is no
advantage in using the LINE INPUT statement over the INPUT statement.

String Manipulation

LEFT$, MID$, and RIGHT$

These three functions are useful for examining a section or substring of a string variable. They allow the user to examine or extract one

or more contiguous characters beginning at the left or right end of a string, or somewhere in the middle.

LEFT$(S$,n) is a function that returns the n leftmost characters of the string S$. It might be used in statements like these:

```
10 A$=LEFT$(NAME$,10)
20 IF (LEFT$(ANSWER$,1)="Y" THEN 100
```

The LEFT$ function is particularly useful when only the first part of a string will provide the necessary information. For example, if a yes-or-no question was asked, some people might respond with only the letter "Y," and others with "YES." The LEFT$ function could be used to check for the first character of the string, which would be a "Y" in both situations. Otherwise, the answer could be misinterpreted. If the answer was affirmative, the letter "Y" was entered, and the statement

```
20 IF ANSWER$="YES" THEN 100
```

was used to test the response, the test would yield a negative result, and the program would not jump to line 100 because "Y" and "YES" are not the same.

LEFT$ could prove useful in sorting a large number of names when the computer's memory is insufficient to contain all of the names. If the names contained up to 30 characters, it might suffice to sort by only the first 10 characters of the name. One might create an array of elements containing the first 10 characters of each name by using the function ARRAY(N)=LEFT$(NAME$,10), fitting this array into the available memory, and sorting on this abbreviated array. After the data was sorted, the computer could use this sorting as a basis to reference the complete names still in a disk file and then print the full names. (Remember when sorting names alphabetically, the last name should precede the first name in the string variables.)

MID$(S$,c,n) is a function that returns a substring n characters long beginning with character c (counting from the left) in the string S$. One function of MID$ is to extract information from a string that has several parts. Consider a disk file for farrowing sows that is composed of string variables, each containing a sow's identification, age, date of last breeding, farrowing date, and time of weaning. Each of these pieces or "fields" of information has a fixed number of characters. If the farrowing date was 10 characters long beginning in position 42 of the string, a list could be sorted and printed for all of the sows from first to last due date by using the MID$(SOW$,42,10) function in the sort routine.

The RIGHT$(S$,n) function is similar to the LEFT$ function except that it returns a substring n characters long counting from the right end of the string S$.

LEN(S$)

The LEN(S$) function returns the number of characters (its length) in the string S$. Although this function is not used very often (at least in this author's opinion), it can be useful when input is restricted in length. For example, the user may be requested to select a disk file name for some data being generated. Some operating systems restrict the number of characters allowed in file names. If the user attempts to use names with more than the allowed number of characters an error will occur. If the maximum number of characters allowed was seven, for example, the following statements could be used to ensure the user did not use a name that was too long:

```
300 INPUT "ENTER NAME OF FILE (7 CHARACTERS MAXIMUM) ";F$
310 IF LEN(F$)>7 THEN 300
```

Logical Operators

A logical operator compares the relationship between two expressions or quantities. The result of a logical operation is either TRUE or FALSE. It can also be a 1 or 0. The three common logical operators are AND, OR, and NOT. They are used quite often in conjunction with IF/THEN statements and equalities and inequalities.

In the previous discussion of the IF/THEN statement, the program jumped to the line number following THEN if the expression was TRUE, or proceeded to the next statement in the program if the expression was FALSE. Some occasions require more than one circumstance to be TRUE or FALSE before a particular action is to be taken.

Let's look at a program that controls the feeders in a limited feeding operation. With this program, the computer always knows what time it is and whether or not the feeders are empty. The computer's task is to turn on the feeder conveyor motor for a preset time if a feeder is empty and at least four hours has elapsed since the last feeding time. The variable FEEDER contains the status of the feeders: "empty" or "not empty." TIMER is the time in hours since the last feeding. The program would be as follows:

```
1000 IF((FEEDER=EMPTY) AND (TIMER>=4))THEN 2000
1010 REM PROCEED HERE IF BOTH CONDITIONS NOT TRUE
             . . .
2000 REM JUMP HERE AND TURN ON MOTOR IF BOTH CONDITIONS
       TRUE
```

Two conditions must be TRUE in line 1000 for the program to jump to line 2000. The value of FEEDER must be equal to EMPTY, AND the value of TIMER must be greater than or equal to 4. The AND operator can be used with any number of expressions or quantities, but it will only compare two values at a time. Therefore, how the parentheses are placed in the expressions is very important.

A second logical operator is OR. The result of an OR operation is the statement Y=A or B is TRUE if either (A) or (B) or both (A and B) are TRUE. If line 1000 in the feeder control was changed to

```
1000  IF((FEEDER=EMPTY) OR (TIMER>=4)) THEN 2000
```

line 2000 would be the next line executed after the IF test when the feeder was empty or when the time since the last feeding had been at least four hours. Only one of the two conditions would have to be TRUE.

The third logical operator, NOT, inverts or negates the value of a logical expression or operation. A TRUE becomes FALSE and a FALSE becomes TRUE. NOT always precedes the quantity to be negated. AND, OR, and NOT can be used together in almost any combination. AND and OR are always placed between two values, and NOT always precedes the value.

Following are some examples of logical operators in use. For all cases, A, B, C, D, and E are TRUE, and F, G, H, I, and J are FALSE. The question is to determine the values (TRUE or FALSE) of X1, X2, X3, X4, and X5.

```
X1 = ((A) AND (B OR F)) AND (C AND G)
X2 = (F=G) AND (H=I) AND (A=B)
X3 = ((A OR F) AND (B OR G)) AND ((C OR H) AND (D OR J))
X4 = NOT X3
X5 = NOT((X1 AND X2) OR X3)

X1 = ((TRUE) AND (TRUE OR FALSE)) AND (TRUE AND FALSE) =
((TRUE) AND (TRUE)) AND (TRUE) = (TRUE) AND (TRUE) = TRUE

X2 = (FALSE=FALSE) AND (FALSE=FALSE) AND (TRUE=TRUE) =
(TRUE) AND (TRUE) AND (TRUE) = (TRUE) AND (TRUE) = TRUE

X3 = ((TRUE OR FALSE) AND (TRUE OR FALSE)) AND
((TRUE OR FALSE) AND (TRUE OR FALSE)) =
((TRUE) AND (TRUE)) AND (TRUE) AND (TRUE)) =
(TRUE) AND (TRUE) = TRUE

X4 = NOT TRUE = FALSE

X5 = NOT((TRUE AND TRUE) OR TRUE) = NOT(TRUE OR TRUE) =
NOT TRUE = FALSE
```

PRINT USING

Controlling how and where information is placed on the output device is a very useful tool in printing information. For example, if a financial statement is printed, most of the numbers will represent dollars and cents. It would be highly desirable to have all of the numbers printed with exactly two digits to the right of the decimal point. If the dollar values were one thousand or greater, commas separating each three digits would make the information easier to read. A dollar sign ($) could be placed in front of some of the values to accomplish this.

In other cases, more than two digits to the right of the decimal need to be printed. For example, this would be necessary if one was figuring grain drying costs and the costs were priced to the nearest half cent per bushel. At other times it might be more convenient to express the answers with an exponential when the numbers were very large or very small. Regardless of the situation, it is best to have the capability of printing the information in whatever form and position best meets the user's needs.

The way in which information is displayed is called its "format." Many BASIC interpreters allow format control beyond the semicolon and TAB function. The format controls the number of significant digits printed, inserts commas in numbers, places dollar signs ($) in front of numbers, and expresses numbers with exponential notation. All of these format controls are used with the PRINT USING command.

The PRINT USING function is followed by the format controls located between two sets of quotation marks and followed by a semicolon. The values to be printed follow the semicolon. This function has the following form:

PRINT USING "desired format";list of variables to print

The information between the quotation marks is the formatting information. Any symbols within the quotes that are not valid format controls are printed as literal characters.

To control the number of digits printed, use the number symbol (#). Each "#" represents one digit. The following examples show some different ways the number 123.456 could be printed, depending upon the format control:

```
PRINT USING "###.#";123.456
123.5
PRINT USING "####.###";123.456
  123.456
PRINT USING "###";123.456
123
PRINT USING "###.## gallons per acre";123.456
123.46 gallons per acre
```

Include a sufficient number of number symbols to the left of the decimal for the largest number that will be printed, or an error will occur. The statement PRINT USING "###.#";1234.5 will result either in an error message and no number being printed, or in the number being printed with a symbol (usually "%") preceding it to indicate the number was too big for the format. This is true only for digits to the left of the decimal. Numbers with fractional values are rounded off to fit the format. If negative values are printed, an extra column (#) must be reserved for the sign. A reserved space for the sign is not necessary if the number is positive.

Commas can be placed after each three digits by using a comma in the format field. The comma must follow all number signs to the left of the decimal, but precede the decimal point if it is included. For example:

```
PRINT USING "####,";1234
1,234
PRINT USING "####,.####";1234.5678
1,234.5678
PRINT USING "####.####,";1234.5678
1234.5678,
```

You can see in the last example what happens when the comma is placed to the right of the decimal. The BASIC interpreter did not consider the trailing comma to be part of the format, so it printed it as a literal character.

A dollar sign will be printed before a number if it is placed at the beginning of the format. For example:

```
PRINT USING "$###.##";123.45
$123.45
PRINT USING $#####.##";123.45
$   123.45
PRINT USING "$$#####.##";123.45
    $123.45
PRINT USING "$####,.##";1234.56
$1,234.56
```

In the first example, the "$" immediately precedes the number, whereas, in the second example, there are two blank spaces between the number and the "$." The first example allowed three spaces for the whole part of the number, which was exactly what was needed. The second example specified five spaces for the number, but only three were used. Room was still reserved for the other two spaces, so the "$" preceded the five space field. The third example provides a way to rectify this problem with the use of two dollar symbols in the format. The fourth example shows the comma and the "$" combined in a single format.

By now you may be thinking that there are a lot of bothersome details to remember in formatting, and you are absolutely right. (Remember, the first rule of programming is do not write a program unless you really have to. Now you may begin to understand why.) One of the easiest ways to judge the quality of a program is in the form of the output. A person who has taken the time and effort to center titles, align columns, control the number of significant digits printed, etc., is more likely to have taken the time and effort to do the other parts of the program well, too. Formatting the output is the single most time-consuming chore in writing a program.

The only form we have not discussed is the exponential format. The exponential format is not used as much as the other forms, but is very useful when dealing with very large or very small numbers. It uses "$^\wedge\,^\wedge\,^\wedge\,^\wedge$" after the last number symbol in the format. For example:

```
PRINT USING "##.#^^^^";123456
1.2E+05
PRINT USING "###.##^^^^";123456
12.35E+04
PRINT USING "###.##^^^^";.000000123456
12.35E-08
PRINT USING "###.##^^^^";-.00000123456
-12.35E-07
PRINT USING "###.##^^^^";12345678
12.35D+06
```

In all five examples there is one less significant digit to the left of the decimal than there are "#"'s in the format. One digit is always reserved for the sign. The first four examples use an "E" to indicate the exponential form. The fifth one uses "D" because it is a double-precision number and there are more than seven significant digits in the number 12345678.

Other format controls that have not been discussed include placing a negative sign (−) after negative numbers and replacing leading blanks in a numeric field with asterisks (*). Refer to your computer's BASIC manual if you need these capabilities.

Not all forms of BASIC have the format controls available with PRINT USING. So, when you select a computer system, consider what kind of format controls are available.

Disk commands

The variation in the syntax of disk commands among the various computers is so large, including a specific set of commands here would not be very useful. You will have to learn the ones for your specific system. These commands are part of the disk operating system. The disk operating system controls all communication between the computer's memory and the disks. It commands the drive motors, the read/write head, the disk directory, information transfer, and the opening and closing of files.

All files must be opened before they can be accessed. The two data file types are sequential and direct access (or random access). Sequential files must be specified as being open either for input or for output, but not for both. Direct access files can be opened for both operations at the same time. When all file accesses are completed, the file must be closed. Closing a file precludes any further reading or writing. Files are opened and closed by BASIC commands that provide instructions for the disk operating system.

Sequential files store data sequentially. Each piece of information added to a file is added immediately after the previous one. Sequential files are always read in order starting at the beginning of the file and continuing usually through the last item. Some operating systems allow data to be added onto the end of a previously existing file by a process called "appending." Others do not allow appending, and always start entering information at the beginning of the file. This latter method destroys any information existing in the file before it was opened.

Direct access files can be read and written in any chosen order. An item can be added or read from any location in the file by specifying the location number. Data in a direct access file must be a fixed length. It is the fixed length of the records (pieces of data) that permits them to be accessed in a random manner. Since the operating system knows how big each record is, it can tell where each one is located.

Sequential files can have variable length records, but they can only be accessed sequentially. A sequential file can usually store more data in less space than can a direct access file. One of the major tradeoffs between the two file types is compact storage for sequential files versus single record accessibility with direct access files. Direct access files also require more program steps to ensure that each record has the proper fixed length.

Summary

You have now been exposed to most of the BASIC commands, excluding those relating to disk operations. You are strongly encouraged to experiment with them as soon and as much as possible. Find out what the capabilities and limitations of your system are. Many people are able to write simple programs very quickly. There is a much better chance you will retain these concepts if you use them right away. Otherwise, the concepts probably will be forgotten, and you will have to spend extra time relearning them when they are needed. Also, it is only when you begin actually doing your own programming that you will come to realize what the computer can do for you.

Chapter 6
Machinery management

The next several chapters are devoted to computer applications in specific areas of agriculture. Not all of the agricultural disciplines are represented. Rather, actual computer programs are offered in several different areas to acquaint you with how a microcomputing system can be used. The program listings and a discussion of almost every program is included to aid you in understanding how they work. These programs may offer a starting point for you to create new and more productive ways to use small computers in your own field of interest.

Farm machinery management involves selecting the proper type and size of machines, maintaining the equipment, and minimizing the machinery costs while performing all of the needed farm operations in a timely, effective, and efficient manner. This chapter examines some computer applications as aids in sizing implements, computing depreciation rates, and choosing equipment replacements.

Sizing Farm Machinery

The following farm equipment terms need to be defined before beginning the discussion on sizing farm machinery:

Theoretical field capacity (TFC) • the capacity of a machine when operating with no stops, including turning at the end of a row, stopping to adjust equipment, operator personal time, travel to and from the field, etc. The TFC of a tillage or planting unit is the product of its operating speed and width. Theoretical field capacity is measured in hectares or acres per hour for tillage and planting equipment, and in tonnes, tons, bushels, or bales per hour for harvesters.

Effective field capacity (EFC) • the actual, average operating capacity of a machine. EFC includes time to turn, refill hoppers, etc. Effective field capacity has the same units as does theoretical field capacity. It is a measure of how much land is actually covered per unit of time when all of the stops, turns, adjustments, and other delays are considered.

Field efficiency (FE) • a measure of productive time in the field. FE indicates the relative amount of time spent actually performing the field operation. FE = EFC/TFC. For example, if planting takes eight hours, and three of those hours are spent turning at the ends of the field and refilling the seed and fertilizer hoppers, then five hours are spent actually planting the seeds. The field efficiency would be 5 hours/8 hours, which is 0.625 or 62.5%. Field efficiency will never be 100%. Typical field efficiencies may range from nearly 90% for some tillage operations, down to 50% or 60% for planting operations that require a lot of time for refilling the seed, fertilizer, and pesticide hoppers.

Implement draft (or draft) • the force or pull necessary to tow the implement when it is operating in the field. Draft is measured in kilonewtons or pounds.

Work • a force acting through a distance. Work can be thought of as the amount of energy expended to accomplish a task. For the purposes of this book, work and energy can be used interchangeably. It takes work to lift a bale of hay or to pull a plow. If a tractor pulls a planter with a draft of 500 pounds for a distance of 20 feet, it has done 500 pounds × 20 feet, or 1,000 foot-pounds, of work. It requires 1,200 foot-pounds of work to lift an 80-pound bale of hay 15 feet into a loft. The metric system expresses work in newton-meters, whereas, the English system uses foot-pounds.

Power • the rate of doing work, or the amount of work done per unit time. If the 1,000 foot-pounds of work in the previous definition has been performed in 2 minutes, the power would be 1,000 foot-pounds per 2 minutes, or 500 foot-pounds per minute. The unit of farm power in the English system is the horsepower. One horsepower is equal to 33,000 foot-pounds per minute. The unit of power in the metric system is the kilowatt, which is equivalent to 1,000 newton-meters per second.

Drawbar power is the power available at the tractor drawbar to pull an implement. It is equal to the drawbar draft times the speed at which the implement is pulled. The PTO POWER of a tractor is the power available at the tractor's power-take-off shaft. It is the product of the torque on the PTO shaft and its rotational speed. A tractor's PTO power is always greater than its drawbar power due to power losses in the transmission and especially to tire slippage. Towed implements need drawbar power, but tractors are rated by their PTO power. So, drawbar power must be converted to PTO power when sizing tractors.

Guidelines

The basic criterion for selecting farm equipment is capacity rather than cost. The capacity of a piece of machinery is the rate at which the machinery performs its intended function. For a tillage implement or a planter, the capacity would be rated in terms of hectares (or acres) per hour that the equipment covered. A harvester would be rated in terms of throughput per hour, that is, tonnes, tons, bushels, or bales per hour. For harvesters, this capacity is sometimes referred to as the harvesters' operating or material capacity.

The capacity required for a farm machine is determined by the time available to perform the operation. Some operations are more important than others in terms of timeliness. Timeliness refers to the value of performing an operation at a particular time. Combining soybeans and planting corn are two operations that are very costly in terms of delay. They need to be performed as quickly as possible. Other operations, such as fall plowing and cultivation, are not as critical. The more costly the delay in performing an operation, the greater must be the capacity of the machine. Determining the time available to perform an operation is beyond the scope of this book. The emphasis here will be on how to size the equipment after determining the time available for an operation and defining the effective field capacity. For example, if 120 hectares of corn have to be planted within six working days, a planter is needed with an effective field capacity of 20 hectares per day.

Except for tractors, most farm implements are sized for a particular field capacity. The size of the tractor or other power unit is determined by the implement with the largest power requirement that it will be pulling or operating.

Sample program

Let's go through the steps discussed in an earlier chapter for writing a program:

Step 1. Define problem. A method is needed to select the proper size of tillage implements, grain drills, and row-crop planters.

Step 2. Define results needed. For tillage implements and grain drills, the size should be the width of the implement. A planter should be sized according to the number of rows it can plant. Since it is unlikely the answer will be an integral number of rows for the planter, the program should provide the effective field capacity for the next largest whole number of rows. This will ensure the planting can be finished in time. For example, if the calculated size for a row-crop planter was 4.5 rows, the program should specify a 5-row planter and display the TFC and EFC for the 5-row machine.

It would be helpful if the results included the theoretical and effective field capacities for each implement. A list of the information entered by the user should be included with the results as a check for the user. The answers should be presented in either metric or conventional units, depending upon the system the user prefers.

Step 3. Define information to be entered by user. To define the information required by the program, one must know how the equipment is sized. Let's consider the three classes of equipment sizing separately: tillage equipment and combines, grain drills, and row crop planters or other row equipment (cultivators, sprayers, harvesters, etc.).

Tillage equipment and combines. The theoretical field capacity of a tillage implement is a product of its operating speed and its width. Its effective field capacity (EFC) is equal to the average amount of land covered per unit time—acres or hectares per hour. The EFC is also the product of the theoretical field capacity, field efficiency, and effective width. The effective width of a tillage implement is the fraction of its total width that is actually used for tilling. Some of its total width is lost due to overlap. For instance, a lawn mower may have a blade that can cut a 22-inch swath, but the average strip cut may be only 20 inches. The width actually cut is less than the length of the mower blade because the operator will overlap the swaths slightly to avoid leaving small strips of uncut grass. This situation is true for many tillage implements. In the case of the lawn mower, the effective width is 20/22, which is 0.91, or 91%, and its overlap is 9%. We will assume that planters and grain drills have an effective width of 100%.

Now we can define the inputs. One input is the total amount of land that must be tilled. Another input could be the effective field capacity, but the user probably would not know what the EFC is for a particular implement. However, he should know the speed at which he will be operating his equipment, and how many working days he will have to complete the task. He would also need to know how long a working day is, in hours, and some idea of his field efficiency. He will need to know the amount of swath overlap for tillage tools. These are the inputs selected for the program written here. However, if you think in terms of effective field capacity, you will be able to modify the program to reflect that change.

The inputs required by the program should be in terms that the user understands and knows. Make the program rather than the user do whatever conversions are necessary. The purpose of a computer program is to alleviate the user's need for tedious and detailed calculations.

We have defined the inputs that will be required for sizing tillage equipment: operating speed of the implement; amount of land that must be tilled; number of working days available to complete the task; number of working hours per day; field efficiency; and swath width or amount of overlap.

Grain drills. Grain drills are sized the same as are tillage implements, except the overlap for grain drills is assumed to be zero.

Row crop equipment. A row crop implement can be treated in the same way as tillage implements and grain drills since it too is required to cover a given amount of land per time. In addition to determining the input information required for tillage implements and grain drills, one will also have to specify the row spacing. Row spacing is usually defined in inches or centimeters. Overlap should be zero for row crop implements and grain drills, since all rows should be uniformly spaced.

Step 4. Determine equations and data needed by program. The computer program must contain the equations for calculating effective and theoretical field capacities. It must also contain the conversion factors necessary to calculate the results in either English or metric units. The following equations need to be included in the program to calculate TFC in English units:

TFC (acres/hr) = speed (mph) × width (ft) / 8.25

row crop implement width (ft) = no. rows × row spacing (in)/12.

For harvesters, the TFC would be equal to the TFC in acres per hour multiplied by the harvested yield per acre. The following equations would be necessary to calculate TFC in metric units:

TFC (hectares/hr) = speed (km/hr) × width (m) / 10.

row crop implement width (m) = no. rows × row spacing (cm)/100

For harvesters, the TFC would be the TFC in hectares per hour multiplied by the harvested yield per hectare.

Following is the equation necessary to determine EFC:

EFC = TFC × FE × (1-overlap)

Step 5. Check existing software. No existing software was found to size machinery.

Step 6. Estimate time needed to write program. The author estimated two hours to write the program. It took eight hours.

Step 7. Write program.

Make a flowchart. Figure 6-1 is a flowchart for an equipment sizing program.

Write in modules. Refer to Machinery Listing 1 for the following discussion. The program starts with line 100, and is divided into modules as described in the following section.

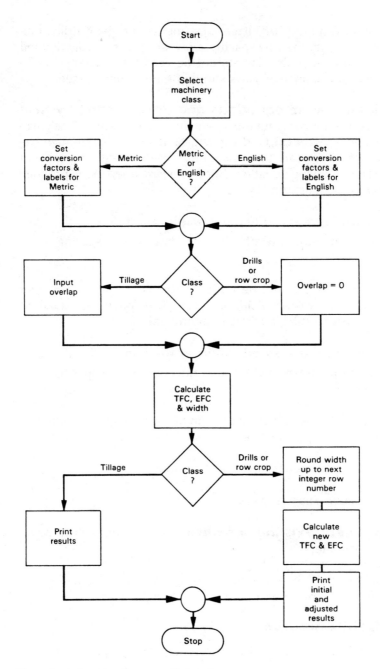

Figure 6-1 • Flowchart for Equipment Sizing Program

Machinery Listing 1 • Farm Equipment Sizing Program

```
1  '   EQUIPMENT SIZING PROGRAM - F.E. SISTLER 1982
95 '       MENU
100 GOSUB 1640        'PRINT PROGRAM TITLE
110 PRINT TAB(30);"MENU":PRINT
115 PRINT "1 - TILLAGE EQUIPMENT OR COMBINE"
120 PRINT "2 - GRAIN DRILL"
125 PRINT "3 - ROW-CROP EQUIPMENT":PRINT
130 INPUT "ENTER NUMBER CORRESPONDING TO DESIRED CLASS";
    CLASS:PRINT
140 INPUT "ENTER 1 FOR ENGLISH UNITS OR 2 FOR METRIC UNITS
    ";TYPE:PRINT
180 ON TYPE GOSUB 860,1080
200 ' _____
220 INPUT "NUMBER OF WORKING DAYS TO COMPLETE THE JOB
    ";DAYS
240 INPUT "NUMBER OF HOURS AVAILABLE PER WORKING DAY
    ";HOURS
260 INPUT "FIELD EFFICIENCY (PERCENT) ";FE
280 ON CLASS GOTO 320,380,440
300 '       TILLAGE EQUIPMENT OR COMBINES - GET OVERLAP
320 INPUT "ENTER EQUIPMENT OVERLAP (PERCENT) ";OVRLAP
340 GOTO 520
360 '       GRAIN DRILL - NO OVERLAP
380 OVRLAP=0
400 GOTO 520
420 '       ROW CROP EQUIPMENT
440 OVRLAP=0
460 PRINT "ENTER ROW SPACING ";RO$:INPUT ROSPAC
480 '           TILL/DRILL/PLANT
500 '       CALCULATE EFC, TFC AND WIDTH
520 EFC = AREA/(DAYS*HOURS)
540 TFC=EFC/((FE/100)*(1-OVRLAP/100))
560 WIDTH=TFC*CNST/SPEED
580 ON CLASS GOTO 600,600,680
600 IF CLASS=1 THEN CLASS$="TILLAGE IMPLEMENTS OR COMBINES"
    ELSE CLASS$="GRAIN DRILL"
620 GOSUB 1340:GOSUB 1440
640 END
650 ' _____
660 '       PLANTER CALCULATIONS WITH COMPENSATION FOR
    INTEGER NUMBER OF ROWS
680 NROS=WIDTH/(ROSPAC*CVRT)
700 IF INT(NROS)=NROS THEN NUM=NROS ELSE NUM=INT(NROS+1)
710 '       NEW TFC W/INTEGER NUMBER OF ROWS
720 TNFC=SPEED*(NUM*ROSPAC*CVRT)/CNST
730 '       NEW EFC W/INTEGER NUMBER OF ROWS
740 ENFC=TNFC*(FE/100)
760 GOSUB 1640
780 CLASS$="ROW CROP EQUIPMENT"
800 GOSUB 1340:GOSUB 1500
820 END
```

```
840 ' ------------------------------------------------
850 '            ENGLISH UNITS CONVERSION CONSTANTS
860 CNST=8.25
880 INPUT "ENTER TOTAL NUMBER OF ACRES TO COVER ";AREA
900 OS$="MILES PER HOUR"
920 INPUT "ENTER OPERATING SPEED IN MILES PER HOUR ";SPEED
940 WIDTH$=" FEET"
980 FC$=" ACRES/HOUR"
1000 RO$=" INCH"
1020 CVRT=1./12.
1040 RETURN
1060 ' ------------------------------------------------
1070 '       METRIC UNITS CONVERSION CONSTANTS
1080 CNST=10
1100 INPUT "TOTAL NUMBER OF HECTARES TO COVER ";AREA
1120 OS$=" KILOMETERS PER HOUR"
1140 INPUT "OPERATING SPEED IN KILOMETERS PER HOUR ";SPEED
1160 WIDTH$=" METERS"
1180 AREA$=" HECTARES"
1200 FC$=" HECTARES/HOUR"
1220 RO$=" CENTIMETER"
1240 CVRT=1./100.
1260 RETURN
1300 ' ------------------------------------------------
1320 '       PRINT RESULTS
1340 GOSUB 1640                    'PRINT PROGRAM TITLE
1350 PRINT TAB(10);CLASS$:PRINT
1360 PRINT USING "THEORETICAL FIELD CAPACITY = ###.#";TFC;
1370 PRINT FC$:PRINT
1380 PRINT USING "EFFECTIVE FIELD CAPACITY = ###.#";EFC;
1390 PRINT FC$:PRINT
1400 PRINT "OPERATING SPEED = ";SPEED;OS$:PRINT
1420 RETURN
1430 ' ------------------------------------------------
1440 PRINT USING "AN IMPLEMENT WIDTH OF ###.#";WIDTH;
1445 PRINT WIDTH$;" IS REQUIRED"
1446 PRINT "TO COVER ";AREA;:PRINT AREA$;" IN ";DAYS:
1447 PRINT "DAYS WORKING ";HOURS;" HOURS PER DAY"
1460 PRINT "WITH A FIELD EFFICIENCY OF ";FE;" PERCENT":PRINT
1480 RETURN
1490 ' ------------------------------------------------
1500 PRINT USING "A ###.# ";NROS;
1505 PRINT USING " ROW PLANTER WITH ###.#";ROSPAC;PRINT
     RO$;
1510 PRINT " ROW SPACING IS REQUIRED"
1511 PRINT "TO PLANT ";AREA;:PRINT AREA$;" IN ";DAYS;
1512 PRINT "DAYS WORKING ";HOURS;" HOURS PER DAY"
1520 PRINT "WITH A FIELD EFFICIENCY OF ";FE;" PERCENT":
     PRINT
1540 PRINT "RECOMMEND USING A ";NUM;" ROW PLANTER WITH ";
1545 PRINT ROSPAC;RO$;" ROW SPACING":PRINT
1560 PRINT USING "IT WOULD HAVE A THEORETICAL CAPACITY OF
     ###.#";TNFC;:PRINT FC$
```

```
1580 PRINT USING "AND AN EFFECTIVE FIELD CAPACITY OF
     ###.#";ENFC;
1590 PRINT FC$
1600 PRINT "AT THE SAME SPEED AND FIELD EFFICIENCY"
1605 NEDAYS=AREA/(ENFC*HOURS)
1610 PRINT USING "JOB WOULD BE COMPLETED IN ###.#
     DAYS";NEDAYS
1620 RETURN
1630 ' ---------------------------------------------------
1640 CLS:PRINT TAB(20);"*** EQUIPMENT SIZING PROGRAM ***"
1650 PRINT
1660 RETURN
```

Document program.   In the program listing, everything to the right of an apostrophe is a comment for the person reading the program listing. Some forms of the BASIC language use the word REM to signify that whatever else follows it on the same line number is to be treated as remarks or comments and is to be ignored by the command interpreter. (The command interpreter takes each line in a computer program and "interprets" it so the computer can understand what it is supposed to do.) The comments and the dashed lines are used to divide the program into sections and to explain the various conversion factors and equations.

Internal documentation is documentation contained within the actual program listing. External documentation refers to manuals or other materials supplied with a program that explains how the program works or how it should be used. Part of ensuring good internal documentation is choosing variable names that serve as descriptors for their roles in the program. For instance, there are three possible classes of implements: tillage tools, grain drills, and planters. Therefore the variable used to store the implement class is called CLASS. TFC is used as a variable name to store the theoretical field capacity, EFC is the effective field capacity, etc. Descriptive variable names should be chosen whenever possible.

Make output neat and complete.   The printed results include the inputs, the calculated width, and the theoretical and effective field capacities. The inputs are included in the output to provide a way of checking for typographical errors.

The program could also provide for printing the results on a printer if needed. If you wish to send the results to a printer, substitute "LPRINT" for "PRINT" in the results section of the program.

Write logically.   The first section requests the necessary inputs, the next section calculates the results, and the last section prints the results.

Make it friendly.   The user is told what form the response should take—inches, centimeters, hours, etc. The output includes units in each step of the results to make it easier to understand. Since the program was so short, no input error-checking routines were included. With short programs that require only a small amount of data entry, it is easier to rerun the program than it is to write complex error-checking routines. Friendly programs always take much longer to write because of the extra information on their use provided within the program. They also take longer to check for valid responses by the user.

Step 8. Debug and validate program. The program was run for all three classes of implements with both English and metric units for each class. The results were compared to hand-calculated answers, and they agreed. In very complex programs, it is often difficult to test for all possible cases or input combinations. But whenever possible, test every case. Making assumptions about how a program will respond in an unverified condition is very risky. The program is now complete and ready to use.

Discussion of program

Lines 100–180 notify the user what program is being run and determine the equipment class and the system of units to be used. Lines 220–620 request the user for the necessary information to size the equipment, then the computer calculates the results. Lines 660–820 determine the number of rows for a row crop implement, then converts the implement's size to an integer number of rows by rounding up to the next integer number. The program then calculates the new theoretical and effective field capacities for the integer row value.

Lines 840–1260 contain subroutines that define appropriate constants and labels for either an English or a metric measurement system. Lines 1320–1660 comprise the section in which the results are printed.

Equipment Depreciation

Three commonly used methods for calculating equipment depreciation are the straight line, the sum-of-the digits, and the declining balance. Each method has certain advantages. The equipment manager may want to examine the depreciation rates for all three methods to select the one most profitable for a particular situation.

In the following discussion, "economic life," as defined by Hunt, is "the length of time from purchase of a machine to that point where it is more economic to replace with a second machine than to continue with the first" (Hunt, Donell. *Farm Power and Machinery Management*. Ames,

Ia.: Iowa State Univ., 1977). "Salvage value" refers to the value of the machine at the end of its economic life. "Purchase price" is the price actually paid for the machine.

Sample program

Step 1. Define problem. Depreciation for several pieces of farm equipment need to be calculated with all three methods of depreciation.

Step 2. Define results needed. The results should contain for each method the beginning value, ending value, and amount of depreciation for each year of the machine's economic life.

Step 3. Define information to be entered by user. The user must enter a description of the equipment, the year it was purchased, the purchase price, the estimated salvage value, and the economic life of the machine.

Step 4. Determine data and formulas needed for program. The program must contain the formulas or algorithms for calculating all three depreciation methods.

Straight-line method. With the straight-line depreciation method, the annual depreciation is equal to the machine's total depreciation divided by its economic life. The total depreciation is the cost of the machine less its salvage value:

$$\text{Annual depreciation} = (C - S)/L$$

where

      C = purchase price (cost)

      S = salvage value

      L = economic life of machine in years.

Sum-of-the-digits method. In sum-of-the-digits method, depreciation in any year, n, of a machine's economic life is the total depreciation of the machine multiplied by its economic life, L, less n, and divided by the sum of the digits from one to L:

$$\text{Depreciation (year n)} = (C-S)*(L-n)/(1+2+3+\ldots+n)$$

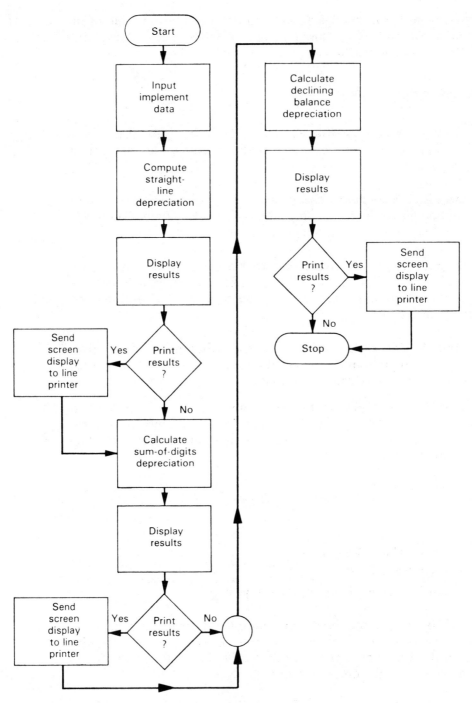

Figure 6-2 • Flowchart for Equipment Depreciation Program

Declining balance method. The declining-balance method computes the machine's value at the end of year n by multiplying the purchase price by (1−R/L), and raising it to the power n, where R is the rate of depreciation and L is the economic life of the machine. R will have an assumed value of 2. The value of R can be changed by changing its value in line 170 of the program.

Remaining value (end of year n) = ((1−R/L) * C)^(n−1).

Step 5. Recheck existing software. Assume none could be found.

Step 6. Estimate time needed to write program. The estimated time was three hours. The actual writing time was six hours.

Step 7. Write program.

Make a flowchart. Figure 6-2 is a flowchart for an equipment depreciation program.

Machinery Listing 2 • Equipment Depreciation Program

```
1 '       EQUIPMENT DEPRECIATION PROGRAM - F.E. SISTLER
100 CLS:PRINT TAB(15);"*** EQUIPMENT DEPRECIATION PROGRAM
    ***":PRINT
110 S$="$$######,.##"
120 INPUT "DESCRIPTION OF EQUIPMENT ";D$:PRINT
130 INPUT "YEAR PURCHASED (4 DIGIT NUMBER) ";YEAR:PRINT
140 INPUT "PURCHASE PRICE ";PURCHASE:PRINT
150 INPUT "ECONOMIC SERVICE LIFE (NUMBER OF YEARS) ";SERVICE
    :PRINT
160 INPUT "SALVAGE VALUE ";SALVAGE:PRINT
170 R=2  'DEPRECIATION RATE - DECLINING BALANCE
180 CLS
190 ' -----------------------------------------------------
200 '          STRAIGHT LINE METHOD OF DEPRECIATION
220 TYPE$="STRAIGHT LINE DEPRECIATION - "
230 DEP=(PURCHASE-SALVAGE)/SERVICE
240 GOSUB 710
250 GOSUB 720
260 FINAL=PURCHASE
270 FOR Y=YEAR TO YEAR+SERVICE-1
280 INITIAL=FINAL
285 FINAL=INITIAL-DEP
290 REMAIN=INITIAL-DEP
300 GOSUB 770
310 NEXT Y
320 GOSUB 710
```

```
330 INPUT "ENTER P TO PRINT RESULTS OR N TO CONTINUE TO NEXT
    METHOD ";Q$
335 IF Q$="P" THEN SYSTEM "SCREEN"   'RESULTS ==> PRINTER
340 CLS
350 ' ----------------------------------------------------------
360 '             SUM OF DIGITS METHOD OF DEPRECIATION
380 TYPE$="SUM OF DIGITS DEPRECIATION - "
390 SUM=0
395 FOR I=1 TO SERVICE:SUM=SUM+I:NEXT I
400 GOSUB 710
410 GOSUB 720
420 D=PURCHASE-SALVAGE                    'D IS TOTAL DEPRECIATION
430 Y=YEAR
440 FINAL=PURCHASE
450 FOR I=SERVICE TO 1 STEP -1
460 DEP=D*I/SUM
470 INITIAL=FINAL
475 FINAL=INITIAL-DEP
480 GOSUB 770
490 Y=Y+1
500 NEXT I
510 GOSUB 710
520 INPUT "ENTER P TO PRINT RESULTS OR N TO CONTINUE TO NEXT
    METHOD ";Q$
525 IF Q$="P" THEN SYSTEM "SCREEN"          ' RESULTS ==> PRINTER
530 CLS
540 ' ----------------------------------------------------------
550 '        DECLINING BALANCE METHOD OF DEPRECIATION
570 TYPE$="DECLINING BALANCE METHOD - "
580 Y=YEAR
585 FINAL=PURCHASE
590 GOSUB 710
600 GOSUB 720
610 FOR I=1 TO SERVICE
620 INITIAL=FINAL
630 FINAL=PURCHASE*(1-R/SERVICE)^I
640 DEP=INITIAL-FINAL
650 GOSUB 770
660 Y=Y+1
670 NEXT I
680 GOSUB 710
690 INPUT "ENTER P TO PRINT RESULTS OR Q TO QUIT ";Q$
695 IF Q$="P" THEN SYSTEM "SCREEN"   ' RESULTS ==> PRINTER
700 END
705 ' ----------------------------------------------------------
706 '        PRINT LINE OF DASHES
710 PRINT:PRINT STRING$(75,"-"):PRINT
717 RETURN
719 ' ----------------------------------------------------------
720 PRINT D$:PRINT
730 PRINT TYPE$;SERVICE;" YEAR SERVICE LIFE":PRINT
740 PRINT " YEAR";TAB(12);"BEGINNING";TAB(32);
    "DEPRECIATION";TAB(54);"ENDING"
```

```
750 PRINT TAB(14);"VALUE";TAB(54);"VALUE"
760 RETURN
765 ' ------------------------------------------------
770 PRINT Y;TAB(10);:PRINT USING S$;INITIAL;:PRINT TAB(30);:
    PRINT USING S$;DEP;
775 PRINT TAB(50);:PRINT USING S$;FINAL
780 RETURN
```

Write in modules. The program is written in five modules (see Machinery Listing 2): an input module (lines 100–180), one module for each of the three methods of calculating depreciation (lines 200–340, 360–530, and 550–695, respectively), and the output or printing modules (lines 706–780).

Document program. Comments are used to separate and explain the calculating modules, to explain some of the variable names, and to explain the purpose of some of the individual steps in the program.

Make output neat and complete. The output includes a description of the machine being depreciated, the method of depreciation, a yearly summary with beginning and ending values for the machine, and the amount of depreciation during the year.

Write logically. The program listing begins with the input section, followed by the calculation sections, and ends with the printed results.

Make it friendly. The questions asked of the user are self-explanatory as are the results. The program allows the user to obtain a listing of the results on a printer if he or she wants them.

Step 8. Debug and validate. Syntax errors would be immediately evident when the program was run because the computer would stop when it tried to execute any line containing a syntax error. The program is debugged and validated by running it with some test values for the equipment name, purchase price, economic life, and salvage value. When the program runs to completion, the results should be compared with known solutions for the test values. If the results of the program agree with the known solution, the program can be assumed to be valid and is ready to be used.

If the program has more than one set of actions that it can take, be sure to test all of them. For example, the program should be tested for proper actions both when the results are printed on the printer and when they are not. If the program could produce other information such as quarterly depreciation, it would need to be tested in that situation too. Never assume a program will produce valid answers in an untested situation.

Discussion of program

Line 100 contains the program title. Line 110 is used as a format statement. A format statement is used to control how information is displayed on the monitor or other output device. The format statement in line 110 is actually used in the PRINT USING S$ statements in lines 770 and 775. The string S$ is defined as $$#######,.##. The "$$" tells the computer to print a "$" symbol in front of the variable value. The following six "#"'s reserve six significant digits for printing six significant digits to the left of the decimal point. The "," causes a comma to be inserted after each set of three digits to the left of the decimal point to make the number easier to read. The "." followed by two more "#"'s signify that a decimal point is to be printed, followed by two significant digits. For example, if a variable printed with this S$ format had a value of one hundred thirty-two thousand two hundred twenty and thirty three hundredths, it would be printed as $132,220.33.

The sections that compute the three depreciation methods use subroutines for printing the results, since the form for all three methods is the same. Subroutines are used instead of including three sets of program statements, because it requires less memory and is easier to type. Only the title for each method changes, and this is defined in each section with the TYPE$ variable.

The statement SYSTEM "SCREEN" is one computer's (Radio Shack® Model II*) method of sending whatever is displayed on the monitor to the line printer. You may need to change this statement in the three places it occurs to whatever method your particular unit uses for printing the screen information.

The PRINT STRING$(75,"-") statement in line 710 causes a line of 75 dashes to be printed. It separates the depreciation methods on the line printer output for easier reading.

Accelerated cost recovery system

The Accelerated Cost Recovery System (ACRS) was established by the Economic Recovery Tax Act of 1981. It placed depreciable property into groups of 3, 5, 10, and 15 years, depending upon the type of property. The ACRS listing shows a program that will calculate the depreciation for 3-, 5-, and 10-year property for years before 1985. To depreciate for 1985 or later years, change the DATA statements to the appropriate depreciation percentages.

---

*The TRS-80 Model II Microcomputer™ is a trademark of the Tandy Corporation.

Listing for Accelerated Cost Recovery System (ACRS)

```
100 '        ACRS
110 CLS : PRINT "ACCELERATED COST RECOVERY SYSTEM"
120 PRINT : INPUT "ENTER COST OF IMPLEMENT ";C
130 DIM D3(3),D5(5),D10(10)   'ANNUAL DEPRECIATION
140 DIM R3(3),R5(5),R10(10)    'DEPRECIATION RATES
145 ' ---------------------------------------------------------
150 '       READ DEPRECIATION RATES
155 '               3 YEAR DEPRECIATION RATES
160 FOR I=1 TO 3
170 READ R3(I)
180 NEXT I
185 '               5 YEAR DEPRECIATION RATES
190 FOR I=1 TO 5
200 READ R5(I)
205 NEXT I
208 '               10 YEAR DEPRECIATION RATES
210 FOR I=1 TO 10
220 READ R10(I)
230 NEXT I
235 ' ---------------------------------------------------------
240 '       CALCULATE DEPRECIATION
245 '               3 YEAR DEPRECIATION
250 FOR I=1 TO 3
260 D3(I) = C*R3(I)/100.
270 NEXT I
380 '               5 YEAR DEPRECIATION
390 FOR I=1 TO 5
400 D5(I) = C*R5(I)/100.
410 NEXT I
420 '               10 YEAR DEPRECIATION
430 FOR I=1 TO 10
440 D10(I) = C*R10(I)/100.
450 NEXT I
455 ' ---------------------------------------------------------
460 '       PRINT RESULTS
470 CLS             'CLEAR SCREEN
480 PRINT TAB(15);"ACRS" : PRINT
490 PRINT "INITIAL VALUE ";C : PRINT
500 PRINT "YEAR";TAB(10);"3 YEAR";TAB(30);
    "5 YEAR";TAB(50);"10 YEAR"
510 PRINT TAB(2);"1";TAB(10);D3(1);TAB(30);D5(1);
    TAB(50);D10(1)
520 PRINT TAB(2);"2";TAB(10);D3(2);TAB(30);D5(2);
    TAB(50);D10(2)
530 PRINT TAB(2);"3";TAB(10);D3(3);TAB(30);D5(3);
    TAB(50);D10(3)
540 PRINT TAB(2);"4";TAB(30);D5(4);TAB(50);D10(4)
550 PRINT TAB(2);"5";TAB(30);D5(5);TAB(50);D10(5)
560 PRINT TAB(2);"6";TAB(50);D10(6)
570 PRINT TAB(2);"7";TAB(50);D10(7)
```

```
580  PRINT TAB(2);"8";TAB(50);D10(8)
590  PRINT TAB(2);"9";TAB(50);D10(9)
600  PRINT TAB(2);"10";TAB(50);D10(10)
610  PRINT : INPUT "ENTER P TO PRINT SCREEN OR A TO RUN
     PROGRAM AGAIN ";Q$
620  IF (Q$="P" OR Q$="p") THEN SYSTEM "SCREEN" ELSE END
700  ' -------------------------------------------------
710  '          ANNUAL DEPRECIATION RATES (PERCENT)
720  '      3 YEAR RATES
730  DATA 25,38,37        'BEFORE 1985
740  '      5 YEAR RATES
750  DATA 15,22,21,21,21   'BEFORE 1985
760  '      10 YEAR RATES
770  DATA 8,14,12,10,10,10,9,9,9,9   'BEFORE 1985
```

The BASIC program for computing depreciation with the ACRS method has five parts. The first part (line 120) asks the user for the equipment cost and identification. The second part (lines 150–230) reads the depreciation rates for the three methods. The depreciation rates are found in lines 700–770. The next section (lines 240–455) calculates the annual depreciation rate with all three methods for all of the years. The last part (lines 460–620) prints the output. If you always wanted the output to go to the printer, substitute LPRINT for PRINT in lines 480–600.

Equipment Replacement Costs

This section on equipment costs is based upon material in Dr. Hunt's book on *Farm Power and Machinery Management* (Hunt, 77). Farm equipment is replaced because it is obsolete, it cannot be repaired, it becomes unreliable, or maintaining it becomes too expensive.

Obsolescence occurs when a new implement or new technology is introduced that makes the present equipment unproductive or unnecessary. The grain combine made the binder obsolete because the combine could perform more operations more quickly and with less labor. The farm tractor made horse-drawn equipment unproductive because the tractor could handle larger equipment and cover more land in less time.

Whenever repair parts become unavailable, broken equipment must be replaced. It is seldom economical to have parts custom made after the manufacturer stops supplying repair parts for an implement.

A machine's reliability refers to its ability to perform its function without malfunctioning or breaking down. Reliability is concerned with whether or not a machine can be trusted to perform its task in a timely manner. The importance of a machine's reliability is determined by the economic value of the task it must perform. Living with a mower that breaks down frequently may be economical if its primary function is to cut weeds in fence rows and if a cheap source of repair labor is available. A delay in cutting the weeds in a fence row is of little or no economic consequence.

On the other hand, a grain combine's reliability is critical. When the crop is ready to be harvested, every hour's delay is very costly in harvesting losses. The manager must decide how dependable his equipment is, how much more reliable new equipment would be, and what the extra reliability is worth to his operation. (Then he hopes he was right.)

The question becomes "When is the most economic time to replace a particular machine?" According to Hunt, the optimum replacement time for an implement is when the average yearly accumulated costs of a machine are at a minimum and are expected to rise if the machine is kept any longer. The average yearly accumulated cost of a machine is equal to the machine's total costs since its purchase divided by the number of years since its purchase.

The costs include fixed costs (depreciation, insurance, housing, and taxes) and variable costs (repair and maintenance, labor, fuel, oil, and lubrication). Fixed costs are those that are not affected by how much the machine is used. Insurance and taxes have to be paid whether or not the machine is used. Variable costs are a function of use. Fuel and oil are variable costs since their consumption is a direct function of machine use. Twice as much fuel is required to run a machine for four hours as is required for two hours.

The repair and maintenance cost is the factor that could cause increasing costs with increasing age of the machine. According to Hunt, "When repairs (and maintenance) are exactly proportional to use, as in the case for replacement sweeps and shovels for tillage implements, the implement should never be replaced for economic reasons since its accumulated cost per acre gets lower each year of life. But when the repair rate increases with age or use, the accumulated cost per acre does reach a definite minimum period." Any equipment that has an increasing repair and maintenance cost with age should be replaced.

Using the method of average yearly accumulated costs for making equipment replacement decisions will involve keeping records for each piece of equipment. Assuming the appropriate cost data are available, one can develop a program that will keep track of costs for tractors and implements in order to choose the times of replacement.

Still following Hunt's guidelines, the costs will be divided into six categories: 1) depreciation; 2) ISTI (interest on investment, shelter costs, property and sales tax, and insurance); 3) repair; 4) tractor fixed costs; 5) fuel and oil; and 6) labor. Tractor fixed costs, fuel and oil, and labor are not included when the costs record form is used for recording tractor costs. They are charged to the various implements being pulled or

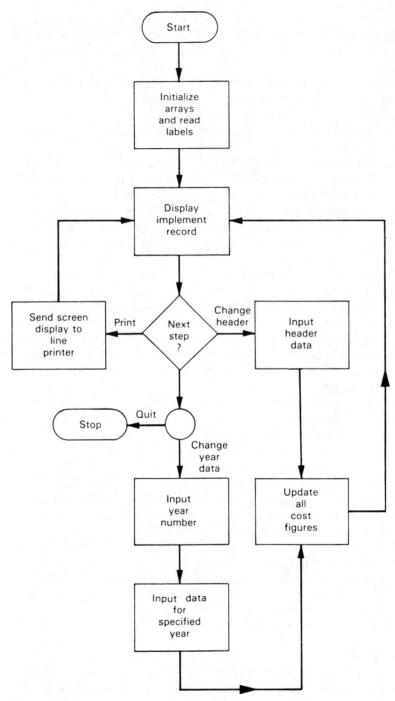

Figure 6-3 • Flowchart for Equipment Replacement Program

powered. A tractor is only productive when it is used with some other implement, so its costs are charged to the implements on a prorated basis.

Sample program

For the sake of illustration, let us assume the replacement will be used for only one piece of equipment. Let us also assume all of the information will be entered at one time, and that the results will not be stored. These are somewhat restrictive assumptions, and the only reason they are made is to keep the program here within a manageable size. The program would be much longer and more complex if data on several pieces of equipment had to be stored and updated.

The following objectives should be met by the equipment replacement program:

1. Allow up to eight years of data for each implement.
2. Allow corrections to be made in any of the data.
3. Calculate yearly cost per acre or hour of use, accumulated cost, accumulated acres or hours, and accumulated average cost per hour or acre.
4. Display the entire record on the monitor.

The flowchart for the program is shown in Figure 6-3. See Machinery Listing 3 for a sample equipment replacement program.

Machinery Listing 3 • Equipment Replacement Program

```
1                EQUIPMENT REPLACEMENT PROGRAM
100 CLEAR 1000 'RESERVE STRING VARIABLE SPACE
110 DIM HEADER$(7)  'HEADER INFORMATION
120 DIM LABEL$(15)
121 DIM A1(7),A2(7),A3(7),A4(7)  'CALCULATED VALUES
122 DIM SUM(7)        'TOTAL COSTS FOR EACH YEAR
123 '      IN REC(Y,Z) Y IS PARTICULAR CHARGE, Z IS YEAR
125 DIM REC(7,7)        'NUMERICAL DATA FOR EQUIPMENT
126 'REC(0,*)=REMAINING VALUE
127 'REC(1,*)=DEPRECIATION
128 'REC(2,*)=ISTI
129 'REC(3,*)=REPAIR
130 'REC(4,*)=TRACTOR FC
131 'REC(5,*)=FUEL & OIL
132 'REC(6,*)=LABOR
133 'REC(7,*)-USE (ACRES OR HOURS)
150 GOSUB 1400        'INITIALIZE & READ LABELS
```

```
170 ' ----------------------------------------------------
290 '        DISPLAY IMPLEMENT RECORD
300 CLS:PRINT TAB(15);"EQUIPMENT REPLACEMENT PROGRAM"
305 PRINT LABEL$(0);SPC(1);HEADER$(0);SPC(2); LABEL$(1);
    SPC(1);HEADER$(1);SPC(2);LABEL$(2);SPC(1);HEADER$(2)
310 PRINT LABEL$(3);SPC(1);HEADER$(3);SPC(2);LABEL$(4);
    SPC(1);HEADER$(4);SPC(2);LABEL$(5);SPC(1);HEADER$(5)
320 PRINT LABEL$(6);SPC(1);HEADER$(6);SPC(2);
    LABEL$(7);SPC(1);HEADER$(7)
330 F$="###### ###### ###### ###### ######
    ###### ###### ######"
340 G$="#####. #####. #####. #####. #####. #####.
    #####. #####."
350 H$="###.## ###.## ###.## ###.## ###.## ###.##
    ###.## ###.##"
360 '        PRINT YEARS
365 PRINT TAB(10);"YEAR";TAB(21);
370 PRINT USING F$;1,2,3,4,5,6,7,8
375 ' ----------------------------------------------------
382 'REMAINING VALUE AT BEGINNING OF YEAR = REM. AT END OF
    YEAR - DEPRECIATION DURING PREVIOUS YEAR
383 REC(0,0)=VAL(HEADER$(4)) 'REM. VALUE STARTS = PURCHASE
    PRICE
384 FOR I=1 TO 7
385 REC(0,I)=REC(),I-1)-REC(0,I-1)
386 NEXT I
400 PRINT "REMAINING VALUE";TAB(21);
420 PRINT USING F$;REC(0,0),REC(0,1),REC(0,2),REC(0,3),
    REC(0,4),REC(0,5),REC(0,6),REC(0,7)
425 PRINT TAB(5);"ANNUAL CHARGES"
426 PRINT "DEPRECIATION";TAB(21);
427 PRINT USING G$;REC(1,0),REC(1,1),REC(1,2),REC(1,3),
    REC(1,4),REC(1,5),REC(1,6),REC(1,7)
430 PRINT "ISTI";TAB(21);
440 PRINT USING G$;REC(2,0),REC(2,1),REC(2,2),REC(2,3),
    REC(2,4),REC(2,5),REC(2,6),REC(2,7)
450 PRINT "REPAIR";TAB(21);
460 PRINT USING G$;REC(3,0),REC(3,1),REC(3,2),REC(3,3),
    REC(3,4),REC(3,5),REC(3,6),REC(3,7)
470 PRINT "TRACTOR FC";TAB(21);
480 PRINT USING G$;REC(4,0),REC(4,1),REC(4,2),REC(4,3),
    REC(4,4),REC(4,5),REC(4,6),REC(4,7)
490 PRINT "FUEL & OIL";TAB(21);
500 PRINT USING G$;REC(5,0),REC(5,1),REC(5,2),REC(5,3),
    REC(5,4),REC(5,5),REC(5,6),REC(5,7)
510 PRINT "LABOR";TAB(21);
520 PRINT USING G$;REC(6,0),REC(6,1),REC(6,2),REC(6,3),
    REC(6,4),REC(6,5),REC(6,6),REC(6,7)
530 '            INITIALIZE TOTAL COST ARRAY
560 FOR I=0 to 7:SUM(I)=0:NEXT I
570 FOR I=0 TO 7
580 FOR J=1 TO 6
590 SUM(I)=SUM(I)+REC(J,I)        'SUM ANNUAL COSTS
```

```
600 NEXT J
610 NEXT I
615 PRINT TAB(21);"————— —————— —————— —————— ——————
       —————— —————— ——————"
620 PRINT TAB(10);"TOTAL";TAB(21);
630 PRINT USING G$;SUM(0),SUM(1),SUM(2),SUM(3),SUM(4),
       SUM(5),SUM(6),SUM(7)
640 PRINT "USE (ACRES OR HOURS)";TAB(21);
650 '          SUM TOTAL COSTS FOR EACH YEAR
670 PRINT USING F$;REC(7,0),REC(7,1),REC(7,2),REC(7,3),
       REC(7,4),REC(7,5),REC(7,6),REC(7,7)
680 PRINT TAB(5);"COST"
690 FOR I=0 TO 7
694 '          ANNUAL COST/use
695 IF REC(7,I)=0 THEN A1(I)=0 ELSE A1(I)=SUM(I)/REC(7,I)
710 NEXT I
720 '          ACCUMULATED COSTS
730 A2(0)=SUM(0)
740 FOR I=1 TO 7
750 A2(I)=A2(I−1)+SUM(I)
760 NEXT I
770 '      ACCUMULATED USE & ACCUMULATED COST/ACCUM. USE
780 A3(0)=REC(7,0)
785 If A3(0)=0 THEN A4(0)=0 ELSE A4(0)=A2(0)/A3(0)
800 FOR I=1 TO 7
810 A3(I)=A3(I−1)+REC(7,I)          'ACCUM. USE
814 '      ACCUM. COST/ACCUM. USE
815 IF A3(I)=0 THEN A4(I)=0 ELSE A4(I)=A2(I)/A3(I)
830 NEXT I
840 PRINT "ANNUAL COST/USE";TAB(21);
850 PRINT USING H$;A1(0),A1(1),A1(2),A1(3),A1(4),A1(5),
       A1(6),A1(7)
860 PRINT "ACCUM. COST";TAB(21);
870 PRINT USING F$;A2(0),A2(1),A2(2),A2(3),A2(4),A2(5),
       A2(6),A2(7)
880 PRINT "ACCUM. USE";TAB(21);
890 PRINT USING F$;A3(0),A3(1),A3(2),A3(3),A3(4),A3(5),
       A3(6),A3(7)
900 PRINT "ACC. COST/ACC. USE";TAB(21);
910 PRINT USING H$;A4(0),A4(1),A4(2),A4(3),A4(4),A4(5),
       A4(6),A4(7)
915 ' ————————————————————————————————————————————————
916 '      PRINT INSTRUCTIONS TO QUIT OR CHANGE RECORDS
920 PRINT @(22,0),"ENTER H TO CHANGE HEADER, P TO PRINT,
       Q TO QUIT"
925 PRINT@(23,0),"OR YEAR NUMBER TO ADD/CHANGE YEAR
       RECORD ";:Q$=INPUT$(1)
930 IF Q$+"P" THEN 960 ELSE IF Q$="H" THEN GOSUB 2000
932 IF Q$="Q" OR Q$="q" THEN END
934 '      CHECK FOR VALID YEAR - ELSE REPRINT INSTRUCTIONS
940 IF VAL(Q$)<1 OR VAL (Q$)>8 THEN 920
950 GOTO 2500   'GOTO MODIFY YEAR ROUTINE
960 SYSTEM "SCREEN":GOTO 300
```

```
1380 ' ------------------------------------------------
1390 '        INITIALIZE ARRAYS
1400 FOR I=0 TO 7
1410 HEADER$(I)="***"
1420 NEXT I
1500 '        READ LABELS FOR CHART
1510 FOR I=0 TO 15
1520 READ LABEL$(I)
1525 NEXT I
1526 RETURN
1530 DATA "MACHINE","MAKE","MODEL","SERIAL NO."
1540 DATA "PURCHASE PRICE","DATE PURCHASED"
1545 DATA "AGE WHEN PURCHASED","YEAR BEGINS"
1550 DATA "REMAINING VALUE","DEPRECIATION","ISTI","REPAIR"
1555 DATA "TRACTOR FC","FUEL & OIL", "LABOR"
1556 DATA "USE (ACRES OR HOURS)"
1580 ' ------------------------------------------------
2000 CLS:PRINT TAB(15);"*** CREATE/CHANGE HEADER INFORMATION
     ***"
2010 PRINT:PRINT "ENTER ALL HEADER INFORMATION"
2020 PRINT "IF YOU MAKE A MISTAKE, YOU CAN CORRECT IT AFTER
     ALL OF HEADER IS ENTERED."
2030 FOR I=0 TO 7
2040 PRINT:PRINT LABEL$(I);SPC(1);:LINEINPUT HEADER$(I)
2050 NEXT I
2060 '        CHECK FOR VALID FORM OF PURCHASE PRICE (NO
     COMMAS OR $ SYMBOLS)
2070 PRINT:PRINT "IS ";VAL(HEADER$(4));" THE CORRECT PURCHASE
     PRICE? (Y OR N)";:INPUT Q$
2080 IF Q$="Y" THEN 300   'IF OK, REDISPLAY UPDATED RECORD
2090 INPUT "REENTER PRICE WITH NO COMMAS OR OTHER SYMBOLS
     ";HEADER$(4)
2100 GOTO 2070
2490 ' ------------------------------------------------
2500 Y%=VAL(Q$)-1
2520 FOR I=1 TO 7
2530 PRINT:PRINT LABEL$(I+8);SPC(1);:INPUT Q$
2531 REC(I,Y%)=VAL(Q$)
2540 NEXT I
2550 GOTO 300   'DISPLAY UPDATED RECORD
```

Discussion of program

The equipment replacement decision will be based upon the values in the last line of the display, which is the accumulated cost divided by the accumulated use. The equipment should be replaced when this value is at its minimum. This is difficult to identify until the cost starts rising again. But, it could enable you to trade before the costs rise too sharply.

At first glance, the program listing may appear a little intimidating. In reality, the bulk of the program is concerned with the appearance of the display and ease of data entry. Only a small part is involved in the actual calculations.

From the flowchart (see Figure 6-3), you can see the overall program control. After the variables are initialized, the entire record is displayed. The user has the options of printing the record on a line printer, changing the header information (equipment make and model, purchase price, date purchased, annual cost and use data, etc.), or stopping the program.

Lines 2000–2540 input the header information. Take a closer look at line 2070. It prints the value of HEADER$(4), which is the purchase price of the machine, and asks the user for verification of the value. The reason for this is that BASIC usually considers a comma in an input line to mean the end of a numeric value. A comma is often used to separate two or more items of data. That means if the number fifteen thousand was entered as "15,000," the computer would only consider the digits to the left of the comma, and it would assume the number was 15. Also, if the number was preceded by a "$" character, such as "$15000," the number would have a value of zero. This test is important since the implement remaining value for each year is based upon the purchase price and the annual depreciation. (See line 383.)

Each time a change is made in any of the information, all of the computed values in the chart are recalculated. This makes it easy for the user to make changes. If, for example, the user meant to add data in year 7, but entered year 8, he or she could reenter the data in year 7 and the results would still be correct.

Now look at lines 695, 785, and 815. In each of these places, the program tests a variable for a value of zero before using it as a divisor. The reason for this is twofold. One reason is that the computer will produce an error message and abort the program if an attempt is made to divide by zero. The second reason is if one of these variables is equal to zero, the data for that year has not been entered yet, so the division would be meaningless anyway.

Lines 916–960 display the user options at the bottom of the screen. The "PRINT@(X,Y)" statements in lines 920 and 925 instruct the computer to print the information following the print statement at a specific location on the monitor. The X value is the line number on the screen (0–23 for the particular computer used here), and the Y value is the column number (0–79). So PRINT@(22,0),SAM would instruct the computer to print the value of variable SAM beginning in the first column of line 22. This form of printing is useful when the relative positions of the rest of the information on the screen need to be left unchanged. In this case, the instructions will be reprinted at the same locations if the user makes a mistake in the data entry. A regular PRINT statement would cause the screen to scroll, and the top lines of the table would be lost. Scrolling refers to adding more lines of information at the bottom of the screen and moving the rest of the information up one line at a time. When the screen is full, the top lines disappear as new lines are added to the bottom.

The end of line 925 has a new form of the input statement. It is Q$=INPUT$(1) instead of the usual INPUT Q$. The latter form requires an ENTER or RETURN key to be pressed after the data entry, which again causes the screen to scroll and lose the top line of information. IN-PUT$(1) tells the computer to stop accepting input after one character on the keyboard has been pressed. This enables the entire screen to be printed if the P key (print option) has been pressed.

The details of these new features have been included here to illustrate some of the situations and problems encountered when writing a program. The features require more work, but make the program easier to use. More time was spent in formatting the screen and the input statements in this program than in writing the computational parts.

Summary

It is hoped that the information in this chapter will give you an idea of what to look for when buying software. Good displays and easy data entry with provisions for correcting mistakes are marks of a well-written program.

Many of the tasks involved in machinery management lend themselves well to computerization. A computer could be used to store machinery use records and to alert the manager when a machine was due for maintenance. It could also size the power units. Tractors and other power units are sized according to the power required by the largest implement or machine that they must operate. The implements are sized first according to their capacity, then the power unit is matched to the capacity. For draft implements, the power would be determined by the draft requirement of the machine multiplied by the speed of the machine.

Chapter 7
Livestock production

Many kinds of information related to livestock production are useful to the livestock manager. Feeding efficiency, or the amount of feed required to add a pound of weight, is a very important factor in poultry and beef production. The swine producer is interested in litter size and rate of gain as well as feeding efficiency. The dairyman wants to monitor milk production and herd health. Some livestock managers maintain their records using manual methods. Some professional groups and businesses provide services to help the farmer with important records. For example, the Dairy Herd Improvement Association provides a computer printout of herd production records, which is mailed to dairymen participating in their program.

If you are considering keeping production records on a personal computing system, commercial software programs are available that may serve your purpose quite well. One point needs to be remembered: Just as much time may be required to create and maintain the records with a computer as with paper and pencil. The advantage of computer-based records will be in the ease with which the results can be analyzed.

The computer can quickly separate all of the dairy cows with milk production below 10,000 pounds per year, or all of the sows that farrowed fewer than eight pigs, or the beef bull that consistently sired slow weight gainers, etc. It cannot extract or produce any information that could not be obtained with other methods. But, since the computer can process and display the information in many forms much more quickly and easily than otherwise possible, the information is more likely to be used.

Animal production records can provide the producer with many kinds of valuable information. Before considering whether to computerize all or part of your records, you should first ask yourself some important questions:

1. What kind of records would help manage the operation most profitably? For example, are individual animal weights important? What about feeding efficiency? Milk production? Litter size? Rate of gain? It is unlikely that the motivation necessary to collect and record the information can be maintained unless the record keeper recognizes a real need for doing so.

2. Will future decisions be based upon the analysis of the records? A set of milk production records can serve as a basis for selecting cow replacements in a dairy herd. If Ol' Betsy is a low producer and lowering the herd average, but is kept because she is the kids' favorite cow, there is no real point in maintaining production records on her.

3. Are you willing to regularly and consistently collect and record the information to maintain an accurate and complete set of records? If not, you may as well stop now. No record-keeping sys-

tem, kept on a computer or on the back of old envelopes, is useful unless it is based upon complete, reliable data.

Farm records are beneficial with filing income taxes and with making economic decisions. Otherwise, they are of questionable financial value.

Sample Production Program Using Sow Farrowing

Like many other livestock enterprises, a sow farrowing operation requires careful management to reach its maximum profit potential. Each sow needs to be bred at the correct time. Missed breeding periods mean reduced profits. The sow must still be fed and cared for until her next breeding period, even though she is not growing more pigs.

The farrowing crate and surrounding area must be ready when the sow is ready to give birth. She must be in the crate (or other farrowing area) when she farrows to minimize infant pig deaths.

Litter size and the litter's rate of growth are important elements in deciding whether or not to keep a particular sow.

As the size of the sow herd increases, it becomes increasingly difficult to ensure that all of the operations and records are maintained and performed correctly and on time. A program that could notify the manager when each sow is due to farrow would be very helpful. To do this, a computer farrowing program would need to perform at least three functions:

1. Recall or read the date each sow was bred and each sow's identification.
2. Calculate the date each sow was due to farrow, and sort the due dates in chronological order.
3. Provide a printed, chronological listing of the sows by due date and identification number.

The ability to store this information for later use (additions, deletions, and updates) would be desirable. This would require adding a section for entering data from the keyboard, and accessing a disk file for reading and writing. The DATA statements would be replaced by the records stored on the disk. An alternate way of storing the information would be to modify the DATA statements in the program whenever sows were added or bred, always saving the newest version of the program.

See Livestock Listing 1 for a sample sow farrowing program.

Livestock Listing 1 • Sow Farrowing Program

```
1 '              SOW FARROWING PROGRAM
2 '
10 ' --------------------------------------------------
11 '        FUNCTIONS FOR DATE CONVERSIONS
12 '
14 DEFFNDV%(A1$,A2%)=(VAL(A1$)>0)AND(VAL(A1$)<13)AND
   (VAL(MID$(A1$,4))>0)AND(VAL(MID$(A1$,4))<32)AND
   (VAL(MID$(A1$,7))>=A2%)AND(LEN(A1$)=10)
51 DEFFNDN!(Y%,M%,D%)=Y%*365+INT((Y%-1)/4)+(M%-1)*28+
   VAL(MID$("000303060811131619212426",(M%-1)*2+1,2))-
   ((M%>2)AND((Y%ANDNOT-4)=0))+D%
52 DEFFNRY%(N!)=INT((N!-N!/1461)/365)
53 DEFFNRJ%(N!)=N!-(FNRY%(N!)*365+INT((FNRY%(N!)-1)/4))
54 DEFFNRM%(J%,Y%)=-((Y%ANDNOT-4)<>0)
   *(1-(J%>31)-(J%>59)-
   (J%>90)-(J%>120)-(J%>151)-(J%>181)-(J%>212)-(J%>243)-
   (J%>273)-(J%>304)-(J%>334))-((Y%ANDNOT-4)=0)*(1-(J%>31)-
   (J%>60)-(J%>91)-(J%>121)-(J%>152)-(J%>182)-(J%>213)-
   (J%>244) -(J%>274)-(J%>305)-(J%>335))
55 DEFFNRD%(Y%,M%,J%)=(J%-((M%-1)*28+
   VAL(MID$("000303060811131619212426",(M%-1)*2+1,2))))+
   ((M%>2)AND(Y%ANDNOT-4)=0))
59 '
60 ' --------------------------------------------------
100 ON ERROR GOTO 200   'GOTO LINE 200 WHEN OUT OF DATA
105 NUM=0
110 READ A$,B$   'READ SOW ID AND DATE BRED
111 IF FNDV%(B$,1984) THEN PRINT "** DATE ERROR -
    SOW ";A$;"** ":END   'STOP IF ERROR IN DATE FORMAT
115 NUM=NUM+1
120 GOTO 110
190 ' --------------------------------------------------
200 DIM BRED$(NUM),ID$(NUM),DUE$(NUM)
205 RESTORE        'BACK TO START OF DATA STATEMENTS TO REREAD
210 FOR I=1 TO NUM
215 READ ID$(I),BRED$(I)
225 '        CALCULATE DUE DATES
230 GEST = 114       'GESTATION PERIOD (DAYS) FOR SOWS
235 M%=VAL(BRED$(I))
240 D%=VAL(MID$(BRED$(I),4,2))
245 Y%=VAL(MID$(BRED$(I),7,4))
250 N!=FNDN!(Y%,M%,D%)+GEST
255 Y%=FNRY%(N!)
260 J%=FNRJ%(N!)
265 M%=FNRM%(J%,Y%)
270 D%=FNRD%(Y%,M%,J%)
275 DUE$(I)=STR$(Y%)+RIGHT$(("0"+STR$(M%),2))+
    RIGHT$(("0"+STR$(D%),2))
280 NEXT I
```

```
300 ' ----------------------------------------------
305 'SORT SOWS CHRONOLOGICALLY BY DUE DATE - SOONEST FIRST
310 FOR I=1 TO NUM−1
315 FOR J=I+1 TO NUM
320 IF DUE$(J)<DUE$(I) THEN SWAP DUE$(J),DUE$(I):
    SWAP ID$(J),ID$(I):SWAP BRED$(J),BRED$(I)
325 NEXT J
330 NEXT I
340 ' ----------------------------------------------
350 '      PRINT  RECORDS
360 LPRINT TAB(10);"SOW ID";TAB(20);"DATE BRED";TAB(30);
    "DUE DATE":LPRINT
361 FOR I=1 TO NUM
365 LPRINT ID$(I);TAB(20);BRED$(I);TAB(40);MID$(DUE$(I),6,2);"/";
    RIGHT$(DUE$(I),2);"/";
    MID$(DUE$(I),2,4)
370 NEXT I
400 END
500 ' ----------------------------------------------
505 '  DATA STATEMENTS - SOW ID & DATE BRED - MANY AS NEEDED
510 DATA "ISABELLE","10/15/1983"
511 DATA "MAYBELLE","10/17/1983"
512 DATA "JENNIFER","09/25/1983"
                                  . . .
1000 ' ----------------------------------------------
```

Lines 14–55 are functions for date conversions. They are from Rosenfelder's book, *Basic Faster and Better & Other Mysteries* (IJG, Inc., Upland, CA, 1981). Rosenfelder wrote them in the compacted manner shown here to minimize storage space and to minimize execution time of the functions. Please refer to his book for a discussion of the details on how the functions operate (and for many other useful functions).

The function DV% in line 14 is used to check that the breeding dates have been entered properly. All dates are assumed to be entered in the form DD/MM/YYYY, where MM is the month, DD is the day of the month, and YYYY is the 4-digit calendar year. The other functions are used to convert the breeding date to a numerical date; to add the gestation period to the date; and to calculate the month, day, and year of the due date.

The ON ERROR GOTO statement directs the program to transfer to line 200 if an error occurs during program execution. An error will occur in line 110 when the program tries to keep reading data values after all of the data has been read. The program assumes all of the information has been entered in DATA statements. The DATA statements begin in line 510 and continue for as many lines as needed. Each DATA statement contains one sow's identification and the date she was last bred. Each time a sow identification and breeding date are read, a check is made in line 111 for a valid date. If the year is earlier than 1983, or an invalid number is entered, the computer assumes something is wrong. It then prints the last sow's ID and the date in question and stops. It is the user's responsibility to correct the problem and rerun the program.

After an ID and date are read, a counter (NUM) is incremented and the next set of values is read. This continues until all of the records have been read. The ON ERROR statement sends control to line 200, and two arrays are dimensioned equal to the number of sows. The RESTORE statement allows the DATA statements to be read again, beginning with the first DATA statement in the program. This time the IDs and breeding dates are stored in the arrays.

As the values are placed in their respective arrays, the due dates are calculated (lines 235–275). After all the due dates have been calculated, they are sorted chronologically with the first sow due placed at the beginning of the list. Lines 310–330 perform the sorting. The sorting method used here is called "bubble sorting."

In bubble sorting (see chapter 5), the due dates listed are compared one by one with the next one in the list. If the second value is less than the first, the two values are exchanged, or "swapped," by the SWAP DUE$(J),DUE$(I) statement. This continues until no more exchanges can be made.

It is easy to add or delete sows with this program. Simply add, modify, or delete DATA statements. Modifications are simplest if each DATA statement only contains information on one sow, although the program could handle multiple sows per DATA statement.

This program could be readily adapted to use with other animals. The only change required is to use the appropriate gestation period defined in line 230. You might also want to change the titles to the appropriate animals.

An alternate way of maintaining the records would be to use a disk file instead of DATA statements. This method has not been included here because changing disk file records is a complex procedure and because different computers use a wide variety of commands to access disk files.

The bubble sorting technique and the DATA statement method of storing information could also be used in many other situations. For example, a similar program without the date functions could be used to sort dairy cows by production levels. Each cow would have an ID and a production level listed, and the list would be bubble sorted by production level. A similar program could be used for litter sizes. In fact, almost any kind of information that is gathered in a random manner but needs to be examined as an ordered set can be kept using some variation of this sow farrowing program.

Charting Market Prices

An obvious factor that affects the profitability of many lifestock operations is the selling price of the animals. Prices are affected by many factors. In some situations, prices are cyclical. This factor could be used in planning for animals to be at their marketing weight when the market is at its peak. Sometimes trends showing how prices vary with time are more easily recognized in graphical form than by looking at columns of numbers.

Let us consider a program that would provide us with a graph of market price as a function of time. We will assume that a time period is equal to one week, although it could be a day, a month, or any other period suited to our purpose. The program must first be able to read the data then to print it in a graphical form.

See Livestock Listing 2 for a sample market price charting program.

Livestock Listing 2 • Market Price Charting Program

```
10 '              MARKET PRICE CHARTING PROGRAM
15 '
100 CLS
110 PRINT "*** MARKET PRICE CHARTING PROGRAM ***"
120 PRINT
125 LINEINPUT "ENTER COMMODITY TO BE PLOTTED ";C$
130 LINEINPUT "ENTER DATE OF FIRST WEEK ";D$
131 INPUT "ENTER LOWEST INTEGER VALUE TO BE PLOTTED ";LOW%
132 INPUT "ENTER LARGEST INTEGER VALUE TO BE PLOTTED ";HIGH%
133 RANGE=HIGH%-LOW%
134 TICS=48 'NUMBER OF DIVISIONS IN THE GRAPH
135 RES=RANGE/TICS   'RESOLUTION OF GRAPH
136 GOTO 180
140 ' ----------------------------------------------
145 '              SUBROUTINE TO PRINT TOP/BOTTOM EDGE OF
    GRAPH
146 '
158 LPRINT TAB(8);
163 FOR I=0 TO TICS/4-1
164 LPRINT USING "### ";LOW%+I*RES*4;
165 NEXT I
166 LPRINT
167 RETURN
170 ' ----------------------------------------------
175 '       PRINT TOP EDGE OF GRAPH
180 GOSUB 158
181 LPRINT TAB(10);
    "+ + + + + + + + + + + +"
185 '              READ DATA AS LOW, AVERAGE, & HIGH VALUES
186 '              LOW=0 ==> END OF DATA
190 WEEK%=0
```

```
210 READ LOW,AVG,HIGH
215 WEEK%=WEEK%+1
220 IF LOW=0 THEN 400   'FINISH GRAPH WHEN OUT OF DATA
225 ' ------------------------------------------------------
226 '                 CALCULATE PRINTING LOCATIONS
227 '
230 L%=10+(LOW)*TICS/RANGE
240 A%=10+(AVG)*TICS/RANGE
250 H%=10+(HIGH)*TICS/RANGE
255 ' ------------------------------------------------------
256 '              SET PRINTING SYMBOLS FOR LOW AVERAGE HIGH
257 '
260 L$="L"
270 A$="A"
280 H$="H"
290 IF L%=A% THEN L$="*":A$="*"   'PRINT * IF VALUES OVERLAP
300 IF A%=H% THEN H$="*"   'PRINT * IF VALUES OVERLAP
310 LPRINT "WEEK";WEEK%;TAB(9);"I";TAB(L%);L$;
311 IF L$<>A$ THEN LPRINT TAB(A%);A$;
312 IF A$<>H$ THEN LPRINT TAB(H%);H$;
313 LPRINT
315 ' ------------------------------------------------------
316 '              GET NEXT SET OF DATA POINTS
320 GOTO 210
390 ' ------------------------------------------------------
395 '              PLOT BOTTOM OF EDGE OF GRAPH & TITLE
400 LPRINT TAB(9);"I";STRING$(48,"-")
405 LPRINT TAB(10);
    "+ + + + + + + + + + +"
410 GOSUB 158
420 LPRINT
430 LPRINT TAB(5);C$;SPC(2);
440 LPRINT "WEEKLY LOWS, AVERAGES, AND HIGHS"
450 LPRINT TAB(10);"BEGINNING THE WEEK OF ";D$
460 END
500 ' ------------------------------------------------------
505 'DATA STATEMENTS HERE - EACH LINE HAS LOW,AVERAGE,HIGH
506 '        VALUES SEPARATED BY COMMAS OR SPACES
507 DATA 10,12,15
508 DATA 9,13,16
                          . . .
1000 DATA 0,0,0         'END OF DATA MARKER
```

The output of the price charting program is sent to the line printer of the screen. This allows a much larger chart to be plotted than could fit on the screen at one time. Using the line printer, there is no limitation on the chart's length except for the number of DATA statements that can be contained within the computer's memory. Even this limitation could be circumvented if the information was kept in a disk file instead of in DATA statements within the program itself.

The prices are assumed to be weekly lows, averages, and highs, but daily values could just as easily be used. To plot daily prices, change the word "WEEK" in lines 130, 310, and 450 to "DAY," and the word "WEEK-LY" in line 440 to "DAILY."

The user is required to enter a commodity identification (steers, calves, wheat, etc.) and the date of the first entry. This information is not processed, but is printed with the chart for ease of identification. The two other values requested are the low and high values for the chart. If these will never or very seldom change, the INPUT statements in lines 131 and 132 could be deleted and replaced with statements that defined these minimum and maximum values. If the minimum was 5 and the maximum was 50, they would be as follows:

```
131 LOW%=5
132 HIGH%=50
```

The program needs these quantities to plot the data points. The range, or resolution, is the smallest change that can be resolved on the plotter. That is a limitation of the plotter. If, for example, there were 100 usable horizontal plotting positions on the printer paper, the resolution would be 1/100th of the difference between the minimum and maximum values plotted. If the minimum was $0.0, and the maximum was $50., the resolution would be 50 cents. The number of plotting positions is defined by the variable TICS, and is set equal to 48 in the example program. (Tic marks are small marks on the vertical or horizontal axis of a graph. They are used to indicate the incremental values of the graph and make the graph easier to read.) The value of TICS should be compatible with whatever printer will be used.

The price axis is labelled in statements 158–166. Every fourth printing position is labelled on both the top and the bottom edges of the graph. The print format used is an integer form, so the values printed will be rounded to the nearest whole number. It is possible to print decimal values by changing the PRINT USING format, but the values would probably have to be printed farther apart than they presently are.

Lines 181 and 405 print a series of plus symbols (+) to indicate the actual positions of the price axis numbers.

The physical printing locations are formed in lines 230, 240, and 250. The values of L%, A%, and H% represent the print locations of the weekly low, average, and high market prices, respectively. They will always be integer values. If there are no coincidental printing locations, the low market price symbol is an "L," the average price is an "A," and the high market price is an "H."

Lines 290 and 300 check for coinciding print locations. Any two market prices that would normally be printed at the same location are printed by an asterisk (*).

Some of the concepts used in this program could be used in other graphical programs. For instance, a histogram program could be written with each histogram bar printed in a manner similar to the market prices. With a histogram, a series of asterisks or other symbols could be printed from the left of the chart up to the value of the bar. The maximum bar value would be computed in the same way as L%, A%, and H%.

To plot on the screen instead of on the printer, change all of the LPRINT statements to PRINT statements. It is usually easier to print values horizontally on a screen or printer than it is to print them vertically. This is because the PRINT statement is oriented horizontally rather than vertically.

Summary

This chapter has provided a flavor of some ways that the computer can help in a livestock operation. Many livestock programs are available for several different microcomputers. Some of the more common ones are for dairy, beef, hog, or chicken operations. When choosing one for your operation, examine it using the guidelines in chapter 2.

Chapter 8

Crop production

The manager of a cropping enterprise is concerned with maximizing long-term profits by optimizing his or her production level while preserving, maintaining, and improving the soil.

Wise managers know that they must have good soil to grow good crops and that lost soil is irretrievable. The soil must be preserved. Soil erosion must be minimized. Cover crops may need to be grown to reduce wind and water erosion. The soil fertility level must be kept high to maintain a high level of production. Crop rotation schedules must be established and followed to prevent the buildup of insects and plant diseases and to improve the soil tilth and fertility. In more arid regions, the land may have to be left fallow part of the time to preserve the soil moisture. Some areas may need irrigation systems, other areas may require drainage systems, and still other areas may need both irrigation and drainage.

Crop production has to be considered from a relatively long-term perspective. Just considering how much money can be made in any one growing season is not enough. One has to make decisions based upon what is best in the long run. The computer can help with some of these decisions, but not with all of them. A machine cannot tell managers if they should use some of their resources to preserve land for future generations. It cannot tell them the social or environmental costs of chemical pollution caused by runoff from the land. But, the computer can keep good records. It can help to evaluate the profitability of a given production situation. It can help managers keep track of what is necessary to produce their crops and of field activities. It can tell them whether or not they are actually making a profit.

Crop production can be viewed from different perspectives. One perspective is from that of the crop. All data related to one crop is maintained as a unit. This includes production costs (machinery costs, labor, fertilizer, etc.), fertilizer applications, pesticides, weather data, and crop yields. Production records help the manager decide which crops to grow when the amount of available labor or machinery changes. They can also indicate which crops are the most profitable and which crop might give the greatest increase with given inputs.

A second point of view is from that of the individual field. Records on individual fields include soil tests, fertilizer applications, irrigation and drainage information, and crop rotations. Field records are very useful. For example, some herbicides have long residual actions that preclude planting certain crops for a period after they have been applied.

Three computer programs will be presented in the remainder of this chapter. One is a cost of production program for grain, a second is for plant population calculations, and the third is a field records program.

Grain Production Costs

The profit, or return to management, will be defined as the difference between the total production costs and the income received from the sale of the grain. The production costs include both fixed and variable costs.

Fixed costs

Fixed costs are those costs that are independent of the production level and occur whether or not a crop is actually produced. Insurance on equipment and on the crop itself, land taxes, interest on the money invested in the land, and equipment depreciation are considered fixed costs. The interest on investment is considered a fixed cost since this money could be otherwise invested to produce an income.

Machinery depreciation will be considered a fixed cost in this program, although it can be argued that depreciation is a function both of time and of use. Repair and maintenance will be considered a fixed cost since the amount of machinery use is assumed to be a constant and is a function of land amount and crop type rather than production level. Machinery costs will be equally distributed over the total number of acres on which each particular implement is used. For example, if a cultivator depreciates $800, and is used to cultivate a total of 400 acres, with an estimated repair cost of $200, the cultivator fixed costs would be ($800 + $200)/400 acres, or $2.50 per acre. Each implement should be considered separately, since some of them may be used on more acres than will others.

The insurance should include the crop's share of the premiums for machinery and for buildings housing the machinery, as well as crop insurance. Sometimes these insurance figures may be difficult to compute. One way to simplify computing them is to subtract the insurance premiums for the family dwelling and other non-crop-related enterprises from the total insurance costs, and divide the remaining value by the number of tillable acres. The reader must use his or her own judgment in determining whether or not to include such things as hospitalization and life insurance on workers. These costs will need to be charged against one or more of the farming enterprises. In many cases, the insurance may not be a large factor in production costs, and not including it may only cause a small loss in accuracy.

Variable costs

Variable costs change with the level of activity. More fertilizer is required to grow 200 bushels per acre of corn than it does to grow 100 bushels per acre. Labor costs increase with the number and level of activities performed on the land and on the crop. Variable costs include labor, seed, fertilizer, herbicides, insecticides, fuel and lubrication, and custom work. Fertilizer and herbicides will be broken into pre- and post-emergence applications. Insecticide costs will be considered one lump sum. This is but one way of dividing costs. Others may be more desirable, depending upon the user's preference. If a particular enterprise would be better served by entering costs in some other form, such as separate entries for anhydrous ammonia and phosphate and for each insecticide application, that part of the computer program could be modified. (The modifications will be discussed in the next section.) Whenever possible, the program should be modified to fit the user's needs, rather than the needs of the user modified to fit the program.

When one is considering the difference between fixed and variable costs, it may not be as important which category the costs are charged to, as it is that all costs are taken into account when calculating the total cost of producing the crop.

The BASIC program shown in Crop Listing 1 calculates the total costs per bushel of grain and the return to management for a given selling price. It also shows the selling price necessary for any specified profit, and the production level required for a specified return to management and selling price.

Crop Listing 1 • Grain Production Costs Program

```
1 '       GRAIN PRODUCTION COSTS
5 CLEAR 1000        'RESERVE MEMORY FOR STRING VARIABLES
95 ' -----------------------------------------------------
96 '              PRINT EXPLANATION OF WHAT THE PROGRAM DOES
100 CLS
101 PRINT TAB(15);"*** GRAIN PRODUCTION COSTS PROGRAM ***"
102 PRINT
103 PRINT "THIS PROGRAM CALCULATES THE RETURN TO
    MANAGEMENT(PROFIT)"
104 PRINT "FOR A GRAIN CROP FOR ANY LEVEL OF PRODUCTION AND
    ANY SELLING PRICE."
105 PRINT "THE REQUIRED INPUTS ARE THE FIXED AND VARIABLE
    COSTS":PRINT
106 PRINT "THE FIXED COSTS INCLUDE:  TAXES, INSURANCE,
    INTEREST ON INVESTMENT"
107 PRINT "(ASSUMED TO BE 12% SIMPLE INTEREST), AND
    MACHINERY COSTS."
108 PRINT "(** NOTE - INSURANCE INCLUDES ONLY CROP
    INSURANCE - PROGRAM MUST BE MODIFIED TO INCLUDE
    OTHER INSURANCE SUCH AS FOR MACHINERY USED IN CROP
    PRODUCTION **)"
109 PRINT
110 PRINT "THE VARIABLE COSTS INCLUDE: LABOR, SEED,
    FERTILIZER, HERBICIDES,"
```

```
111 PRINT "INSECTICIDES, HARVESTING COSTS, FUEL, AND CUSTOM
    WORK. LUBRICATION COSTS ARE ASSUMED TO BE 10% OF FUEL
    COSTS."
112 PRINT
113 PRINT "FOR EACH MACHINE USED, THE USER MUST KNOW (OR
    ESTIMATE) THE ANNUAL"
114 PRINT "DEPRECIATION AND REPAIR COSTS, AND THE TOTAL
    NUMBER OF ACRES ON WHICH"
115 PRINT "THE MACHINE WILL BE USED DURING THE YEAR."
116 PRINT
117 PRINT "FOR EXAMPLE, A PLOW MIGHT DEPRECIATE $700, ITS
    ESTIMATED REPAIR COSTS ARE"
118 PRINT "$125, AND IT WILL BE USED TO PLOW A TOTAL OF 450
    ACRES."
119 PRINT
120 INPUT "PRESS <ENTER> KEY TO CONTINUE ";A$
160 ' ---------------------------------------------------
190 '         DATA INPUT SECTION
200 CLS
205 PRINT "ENTER NUMBER OF MACHINES USED IN PRODUCING THE
    CROP."
210 INPUT "(DO NOT INCLUDE CUSTOM WORK) ";NUM
215 PRINT
220 DIM DEP(NUM),REPAIR(NUM),MACHINE$(NUM),NACRES(NUM)
230 FOR I=1 TO NUM
231 PRINT USING "NAME OF MACHINE NO. ## ";I;
232 INPUT MACHINE$(I)
233 NEXT I
235 CLS
240 GOSUB 1000
250 PRINT "*** FIXED COSTS - ANNUAL DEPRECIATION AND REPAIR
    & MAINTENANCE ***"
255 PRINT
260 PRINT "ACRES REFERS TO THE TOTAL NUMBER OF ACRES ON
    WHICH THE MACHINE WILL BE USED THIS YEAR, INCLUDING ITS
    USE ON OTHER CROPS"
265 PRINT
270 PRINT "MACHINE";TAB(15);"DEPRECIATION";TAB(30);"MAINT. &
    REPAIR";TAB(50);"NO. ACRES"
275 PRINT
276 ' ---------------------------------------------------
278 '          GET DEPRECIATION & USE INFORMATION
280 FOR I=1 TO NUM
285 PRINT@(I+8,0),MACHINE$(I);TAB(15);:INPUT DEP(I)
286 PRINT@(I+8,29)" ";:INPUT REP(I)
287 PRINT@(I+8,49)," ";:INPUT NACRES(I)
300 NEXT I
310 GOSUB 1000
315 ' ---------------------------------------------------
320 INPUT "CASH VALUE OF ONE ACRE OF LAND ";ACRE:PRINT
330 INPUT "ANNUAL TAXES PER ACRE ";TAXES:PRINT
340 INPUT "INSURANCE - $ PER ACRE ";ISURANCE:PRINT
```

```
350 INPUT "ANNUAL HOURS OF LABOR PER ACRE TO PRODUCE
    THE CROP ";HOURS
360 INPUT "LABOR COST PER HOUR ";LABR
370 INPUT "SEED COST PER ACRE ";SEED
380 INPUT "PRE-EMERGENCE FERTILIZER COST - $ PER
    ACRE ";P1FERT
390 INPUT "POST-EMERGENCE FERTILIZER COST - $ PER
    ACRE ";P2FERT
400 INPUT "PRE-EMERGENCE HERBICIDES COST - $ PER ACRE ";
    P3HERB
410 INPUT "POST-EMERGENCE HERBICIDES COST - $ PER ACRE ";
    P4HERB
420 INPUT "INSECTICIDE COST - $ PER ACRE ";P5INSECT
430 INPUT "CUSTOM WORK CHARGE - $ PER ACRE ";P6CUSTM
440 INPUT "GALLONS OF FUEL USED PER ACRE TO PRODUCE THE
    CROP ";GAL
450 INPUT "COST FOR 1 GALLON OF FUEL (DOLLARS - e.g., 1.25
    or 0.65) ";GCST
460 FUELUB=1.1*(GAL*GCST)        'LUBE COSTS = 10% OF FUEL
470 INPUT "ESTIMATED PRODUCTION - BUSHELS PER ACRE ";BPA
480 INPUT "ESTIMATED SELLING PRICE ";PRICE
490 INPUT "DESIRED RETURN TO MANAGEMENT - $ PER ACRE ";RTM
500 ' ------------------------------------------------
510 '        CONVERT ANNUAL FIXED COSTS TO PER ACRE COSTS
520 DIM FXCST(NUM)
540 MACHCST=0
550 FOR I=1 TO NUM
560 FXCST(I)=(DEP(I)+REPAIR(I))/NACRES(I)
570 MACHCST=MACHCST+FXCST(I)        'SUM MACHINERY COSTS
575 NEXT I
580 '        INTEREST ON INVESTMENT
590 INVEST=ACRE*0.12        '0.12 IS INTEREST RATE
600 '        TOTAL FIXED COSTS
620 SUMFX=MACHCST+TAXES+INVEST+ISURANCE
620 '        VARIABLE COSTS
630 VARBL=P1FERT+P2FERT+P3HERB+P4HERB+P5INSECT +P6CUSTM
    +SEED+.(LABR*HOURS)+FUELUB
640 '        COMPUTE AND PRINT TOTAL COST PER BUSHEL AND
    RETURN ON INVESTMENT
650 PERBUSHEL=(VARBL+SUMFX)/BPA
660 GROSS=BPA*PRICE
670 NET=GROSS-(VARBL+SUMFX)
680 ' ------------------------------------------------
690 '            PRINT RESULTS
700 '
705 CLS
710 GOSUB 1000
720 PRINT USING "VARIABLE COSTS = $###.## PER BUSHEL";
    VARBL/BPA
730 PRINT USING "   FIXED COSTS = $###.## PER BUSHEL";
    SUMFX/BPA
740 PRINT USING "TOTAL COST (EXCLUDING RETURN TO
```

```
            MANAGEMENT)= $###.## PER BUSHEL";PERBUSHEL
745 PRINT
750 PRINT USING "SELLING PRICE = $###.## PER BUSHEL";PRICE
755 PRINT
760 PRINT USING "NET RETURN TO MANAGEMENT = $###.## PER
            ACRE";NET
770 GOSUB 1000
780 ' -----------------------------------------------------
790 '        CALCULATE BREAKEVEN SELLING PRICE AT GIVEN
791 '        PRODUCTION LEVEL AND BREAKEVEN PRODUCTION
792 '        LEVEL AT A GIVEN PRICE
800 '
820 MSELL=(VARBL+SUMFX)/BPA
830 MPROD=(VARBL+SUMFX)/PRICE
840 PRINT USING "MINIMUM SELLING PRICE FOR A RETURN TO
            MANAGEMENT OF $###.## PER ACRE";RTM
850 PRINT USING "AT A PRODUCTION LEVEL OF ### BUSHELS PER
            ACRE IS $###.## PER BUSHEL";BPA,MSELL
860 GOSUB 1000
870 PRINT USING "MINIMUM PRODUCTION LEVEL FOR A RETURN TO
            MANAGEMENT OF $###.## PER ACRE";RTM
880 PRINT USING "AT A SELLING PRICE OF $###.## PER BUSHEL
            IS ### BUSHELS PER ACRE";PRICE,MPROD
890 GOSUB 1000
895 END
900 ' -----------------------------------------------------
910 '                PRINT LINE OF DASHES SUBROUTINE
1000 PRINT:PRINT STRING$(70,"-")
1020 RETURN
```

Grain production costs program

The main program starts at line 100 where the program name is printed and use of the program is explained. In a program such as this where the program could ask for the input data in different ways, an explanation of what form the entries should have should be given before the data is entered. For example, if the user expects the insecticide costs to be broken down by the number of applications, he or she may enter the wrong information because the example program here expects the insecticide costs to be entered as one sum.

The section starting in line 200 asks for the number of machines used and the name of each machine. The machine names are used later in the program when the depreciation and repair and maintenance figures are requested and when the results are printed.

All of the data entry is completed by the end of line 480. The next question posed to the user is the desired return to management. That is, how much profit would the manager like to make on each acre. This value is used to calculate both the necessary selling price at the assumed production level and the required production level to achieve this return to management at the assumed marketing price for the crop.

Although the costs and revenues in this program are calculated on a per-acre and per-bushel basis, they could be converted to other units by changing the titles. If costs were entered on a per-hectare basis, the answers would be on a per-hectare basis. The program could be used in a hay production enterprise by changing the selling price to dollars per bale instead of dollars per bushel and by replacing "bushel" with "bale" in the results section. To use the program with forage production, substitute "tons" or "tons per acre" for "acres."

Plant Population

Plant population refers to the number of plants per acre or hectare. The seed population is the number of seeds actually planted per acre or hectare. The plant population in a row-crop farming enterprise is very important. Too few plants decrease yield, and too many plants may result in under-sized stalks or ears and will increase seed costs. The row-crop planter must place the seeds at the proper spacing to obtain the desired population. The seed spacing will be determined by the row spacing, the seed germination rate and the desired final plant stand. The seed germination rate is the percentage of seeds that can be expected to germinate and emerge from the ground surface. The final plant stand means the number of plants that actually emerged and grow to maturity.

Measuring the plant population

To calculate the actual plant population, the number of plants growing in a measured length of row are counted. Based upon this number of plants, the length of row, and the row spacing, the plant population can be determined:

$$POP = (NP*43560)/(RL+RS/12)$$

where

POP = plant population, plants per acre

NP = number of plants counted

RL = length of row (feet) in which NP plants were counted

RS = row spacing, inches

conversion factors used: 1 acre = 43,560 square feet;

1 foot = 12 inches

Determining the seed spacing

The standing plant population is equal to the planted population less the seeds that did not germinate and the plants lost during the growing season. Expressed as an equation, this becomes:

$$SPOP = SEEDS*GERM*(1-LOSS)$$

where

SPOP = standing plant population, plants per acre
SEEDS = seeding rate, seeds per acre
GERM = fraction of seeds that will germinate
LOSS = fraction of germinated seeds lost during
growing season

The seed spacing needs to be such that a desired standing population can be grown. The seeding rate can be expressed in terms of the row spacing, the seed spacing, and a constant factor as follows:

$$SEEDS = (144 * 43560)/(RS * SS)$$

where

SEEDS = seeds per acre
RS = row spacing, inches
SS = seed spacing, inches

Using these two relationships, one can develop an equation to solve for the seed spacing, based upon the row spacing, standing population, germination rate, and losses during the growing season:

$$SS = (144*43560*GERM*(1-LOSS))/(RS*SPOP)$$

To calculate the seed spacing in centimeters and the population in plants per hectare the following constants should be changed: substitute 10,000 for 43560; 10000 for 144; 10 for 12; centimeters for inches; and meters for feet.

This program calculates either the standing plant population based upon a measured plant count in the field, or the seed spacing for a desired population.

Crop Listing 2 • Plant Population Program

```
1 '        PLANT POPULATION PROGRAM
90 ' --------------------------------------------------
95 '              PRINT MENU
100 CLS:PRINT TAB(10);"*** PLANT POPULATION PROGRAM ***"
105 PRINT
110 PRINT TAB(35);"MENU":PRINT
120 PRINT TAB(10);"ITEM";TAB(25);"ITEM"
130 PRINT TAB(11);"NO."
140 PRINT TAB(12);"1";TAB(20);"FIND STANDING PLANT
    POPULATION FOR MEASURED PLANT COUNT"
150 PRINT TAB(12);"2";TAB(20);"FIND SEED SPACING FOR DESIRED
    POPULATION"
155 PRINT
160 INPUT "ENTER NO. OF DESIRED ITEM AND PRESS <ENTER> ";N
165 IF (N>2)OR(N<1) THEN 160
170 ON N GOTO 199,399
190 ' --------------------------------------------------
195 '              FIND POPULATION FOR MEASURED PLANT COUNT
199 CLS
200 PRINT TAB(10);"*** FIND STANDING PLANT
    POPULATION FOR MEASURED PLANT COUNT ***"
204 PRINT
205 INPUT "ENTER NUMBER OF PLANTS COUNTED ";NP
206 PRINT
210 INPUT "ENTER LENGTH (FEET) OF ROW IN WHICH PLANTS WERE
    COUNTED ";RL
211 PRINT
215 INPUT "ENTER ROW SPACING (INCHES) ";RS
216 PRINT
220 POP=43560*NP/((RS/12)*RL)
225 PRINT USING "MEASURED PLANT POPULATION IS #######
    PLANTS PER ACRE";POP
226 PRINT "ROW SPACING = ";RS;" INCHES"
227 PRINT NP;" PLANTS COUNTED IN ";RL;" FEET OF ROW"
230 END
390 ' --------------------------------------------------
395 '      CALCULATE SPEED SPACING FOR DESIRED POPULATION
399 CLS
400 PRINT TAB(10);"*** CALCULATE SEED SPACING FOR DESIRED
    POPULATION ***"
404 PRINT
405 INPUT "ENTER DESIRED STANDING PLANT POPULATION (PLANTS
    PER ACRE ";SPOP
406 PRINT
410 INPUT "ENTER GERMINATION RATE (PERCENT GERMINATION WITH
    NO % SYMBOL) ";GERM
411 GERM=GERM/100.        'CONVERT PERCENTAGE TO FRACTION
412 PRINT
413 INPUT "ENTER PERCENT OF PLANTS LOST DURING GROWING
    SEASON (NO % SYMBOL) ";LOSS
```

```
414 LOSS=LOSS/100.        'CONVERT PERCENTAGE TO FRACTION
415 INPUT "ENTER ROW SPACING (INCHES) ";RS
416 PRINT
420 SS=(144*43560*GERM*(1-LOSS))/(RS*SPOP)
425 PRINT USING "SEED SPACING SHOULD BE ###.#
    INCHES ";SS
426 PRINT "GERMINATION RATE = ";GERM*100.;" PERCENT"
427 PRINT "LOSSES DURING GROWING SEASON = ";LOSS*100.;"
    PERCENT"
428 PRINT USING "FINAL PLANT POPULATION = ###### PLANTS
    PER ACRE ";SPOP
430 END
```

Field Records

Field records provide a history of the uses and activities for a particular piece of land. They can include the uses of the field (pasture, corn silage, wheat, soybeans, etc.) the activities performed in the field (plowing, disking, cultivating, etc.) and chemical applications (fertilizers, insecticides, and herbicides). They might also include changes and improvements and other information about the field such as irrigation, drainage, and soil tests.

Field records are another tool for more effectively managing the land. If yield records are included in a field's history, they might be used to indicate sources of problems. An adequately fertilized field with lower yields than adjacent fields could have a drainage problem. Two similar fields with different levels of tillage and the same levels of production may indicate a way to lower machinery costs by eliminating some of the field operations. Some crops are very sensitive to particular herbicides. It may not be possible to grow corn, for example, in a field that had a powerful grass killer applied the previous year.

The real value of field records depends upon how detailed the records are and upon the manager's ability to interpret and use the information.

Field records program

In its elemental form, a program for maintaining field records needs to do three things: identify the file where the field records are kept, add information to the file, and print the information stored in the file.

To develop this basic field record program, let us assume we have a computer that allows us to have sequential files (records of various lengths, stored one after another in the order in which the records are entered). Let us also assume that an existing file can be opened and records added or appended to the end of the file.

If the terms "open" and "close" in reference to a file of data seem confusing, think of a cookie jar. You cannot take a cookie from the jar or put a cookie into the jar without first removing the jar's lid, or opening the jar. When you replace the lid, you close the jar, and no more cookies can be moved into or from the jar. With a disk file you are doing the same thing, except you are closing or opening disk files and moving data.

Two machines that can handle appended files are the Radio Shack® TRS-80 Model III™ and the Apple II Plus®.* A file is appended by adding on to whatever is already there. If a file has six records and another record is appended to it, the new record becomes the seventh one in the file. Other microcomputer manufacturers make machines with this same capability. In the example in Crop Listing 3, the format will be the one used on the Radio Shack® Model III™. Refer to your computer owner's manual for specific details on your system.

For the Model III, the following program will create, update, retrieve, and print the field records for any number of fields, up to the storage capacity of a diskette.

Crop Listing 3 • Field Records Program

```
100 INPUT "ENTER FIELD NAME ";F$
110 PRINT "ENTER 1 TO ADD INFORMATION TO THE FIELD RECORD"
120 INPUT "ENTER 2 TO PRINT THE FIELD RECORD ";N
130 ON N GOTO 140,220
140 OPEN "E",1,F$   'may need to change for your computer
150 PRINT "ENTER INFORMATION TO ADD TO THE RECORD"
160 INPUT R$
170 PRINT #1,R$       'may need to change for your computer
180 INPUT 'ENTER 1 TO ADD MORE INFORMATION OR 2 TO QUIT ";N
190 ON N GOTO 150,200
200 CLOSE 1
210 END
220 OPEN "I",1,F$ 'may need to change for your computer
230 LPRINT "FIELD NAME ";F$:LPRINT
240 FOR I=1 TO LOF(1)       'LOF(1) is number of records in
       file
250 INPUT #1,R$        'may need to change for your computer
260 LPRINT R$
270 NEXT I
280 CLOSE 1
290 END
```

*The TRS-80 Model III Microcomputer™ is a trademark of the Tandy Corporation. Apple II Plus® is a registered trademark of Apple Computer, Inc.

The advantage of this program is its simplicity. Line 140 opens an existing sequential file to append (add) records to the end of the file or creates a new file if one with the stated name does not exist. Each record of information is added to the file after it has been entered from the keyboard. This continues until the user is finished. Later, when more information is to be added, the same procedure is followed. Whenever the field record is to be printed, the user just specifies the file name, and the program opens the appropriate file, reads and prints all of the records one at a time, and closes the file when finished.

If this program meets your needs, use it in its present form. However, it does have a few limitations that need to be considered.

The program requires you to know the name of the file where you have stored the field record information. One way to get the file names would be to do a listing of the diskette's directory before the program is run. The directory usually includes the names of all of the user-created files on the diskette and their lengths. But when the directory is listed, there would be no description provided about the field records in question other than that which can be inferred from the file names. If the file names for the three fields were CORN1, CORN2, and CORN3, for example, one could easily forget which file represented which field. Using file names that were as descriptive as possible would be helpful. For instance, the file names could be the field locations as marked on a plat map or as located on the farm. The south 40 acres might be in file SOUTH40 and the low section might be in file LOWLAND. The more descriptive a file name is, the more useful it is.

Another limitation to this program is that there is no function to check errors. If you meant to add information to the "F123" file, but inadvertently entered "F132" as the file name, a new file would be created with the name "F132" (unless it already existed), and the new information would be placed in it. There would be no indication that anything was wrong, since the computer was never requested to do anything it did not understand. The problem would only become evident when you tried to print the field record and discovered some of the information was missing. Even then, the computer would not supply any clues as to what happened to the missing data.

A partial solution to this problem is to add program statements that will examine the LOF(1) value after the file is opened. LOF(1) contains the length of the file opened as unit 1. If its value is zero, meaning a new file has been opened, the program could ask the user if it is supposed to be a new file. Similarly, if LOF(1) is greater than zero, the program would ask if the user meant to add data to an existing file. The program could take the appropriate action, depending upon the user's response. This is only a partial solution since it would not prevent the user from adding records to the wrong file which previously existed.

Still another program limitation is there is no way to sort the information. A logical way of separating the information might be by calendar year. For example, what crops were grown in 1982, what chemicals were applied that year, and so on. Since the records are not divided into fields (for example, a date field), and the information can be entered into the records in any order, no chronological sorting is possible. Another useful basis for sorting is by the activity category. One category could be the crops grown. Another category could be the kinds and amounts of chemicals applied. A third category could be the tillage operations. The information would be easier to interpret if broken into categories like these instead of having tillage and chemical information and comments randomly scattered throughout a printout.

A more complex program will overcome these limitations. But before you begin writing a more sophisticated program to give added flexibility and reduce the probability of errors, ask yourself whether or not the extra benefits are worth the extra development time. If records were kept on only one field, the answer would probably be no. If records were kept on many fields, and the program would be used several times, the answer would probably be yes. Recalling one of the first rules of program writing, try to find a commercially available program that handled more sophisticated field records. If such a program is unavailable, begin writing a suitable program by stating your needs, drawing a flowchart, etc.

Summary

Computer programs for crop production are being rapidly introduced to the farming community. They can be used to keep complete field histories, to determine production costs, and to merge records with those of other enterprises to provide a comprehensive analysis of the entire farming operation.

Chapter 9
Chemical application

Some crops consume most of their production energy in the form of pesticides and fertilizers. For example, approximately 70 percent of the energy used to produce cotton is in the pesticides and fertilizers; the rest is in the fuel energy for tillage, planting, harvesting, etc. (Production energy refers to the energy supplied by the producer, and does not include solar energy. It includes the energy used to power all of the field equipment. It also includes the chemical energy applied to the field in the form of fertilizers and pesticides.)

A study on farm chemical applications found the two primary sources of application errors are 1) improper mixing ratios, and 2) improper application rates (A. R. Rider and E. C. Dickey, "Field Evaluation of Calibration Accuracy for Pesticide Application Equipment," in *Transactions of the ASAE* vol. 25 (2): 258–260 (1982), the American Society of Agricultural Engineers, St. Joseph, Michigan). Either problem means the crop is not getting the desired level of fertilizer or pesticide application. Calibrating a sprayer, mixing the chemicals, and operating the sprayer at the proper speed are all very important. Too high of a pesticide application rate can damage the crop, pollute the environment, and waste money. Too low of an application rate will not control the crop pests and will result in reduced yields.

Let us consider some programs to help reduce or eliminate these errors. Our study will include ways of calibrating an applicator, calculating chemical mixing ratios, determining the travel speed of the applicator, and selecting the proper spray nozzle capacity. The discussion in the first section can be applied to both liquid chemicals and wettable powders.

Sprayer Travel Speed Calculation

The speed at which the spray rig should be driven is determined by the nozzle flow rate, the number of nozzles, the spray width, and the desired application rate (amount of material per unit of area). The application rate can be increased by decreasing the ground speed, increasing the number of nozzles per unit length of the boom, increasing the spraying pressure, or increasing the spray nozzle orifice size. In English units the flow rate will be in gallons per minute and the boom width will be in feet. For liquid chemicals, the application rate is usually specified as pints or gallons per acre, and for wettable powders the rate is given in pounds per acre.

The flow rate for the sprayer is the product of the single nozzle rate and the number of nozzles. The theoretical field capacity of the spray rig in acres per hour is equal to the spray width in feet multiplied by the ground speed in miles per hour and divided by 8.25. (See chapter 6 for an explanation of theoretical field capacity.) The application rate in gallons per acre will be the sprayer flow rate divided by the theoretical field capacity. Theoretical field capacity is used instead of effective field capacity because the sprayer is turned off when turning or stopping. Expressed as a formula, the application rate equation becomes

$$GPA = (N*FLOW*60)/(S*W/8.25)$$

where

GPA = application rate, gallons per acre
S = sprayer speed, miles per hour
W = spray width, feet
N = number of nozzles
$FLOW$ = single nozzle flow rate, gallons per minute

The previous equation can be rearranged to solve for the travel speed when all of the other factors are known:

$$S = (8.25*N*FLOW*60)/(W*GPA)$$

A BASIC program to determine the sprayer ground speed is shown in Chemical Listing 1.

Chemical Listing 1 • Program to Calculate Sprayer Travel Speed in Miles per Hour

```
890 '       GROUND SPEED CALCULATION - ENGLISH UNITS
900 CLS
905 PRINT TAB(15);"*** GROUND SPEED CALCULATION ***"
906 PRINT
910 INPUT "NUMBER OF NOZZLES ON SPRAY BOOM ";NUM
920 INPUT "TOTAL SPRAY WIDTH (FEET) OF BOOM ";WIDTH
930 INPUT "FLOW RATE OF SINGLE NOZZLE (GAL/MIN) ";FLOW
940 INPUT "GALLONS PER ACRE OF MATERIAL TO BE APPLIED ";GPA
950 PRINT
980 SPEED = (8.25*NUM*FLOW*60.)/(WIDTH*GPA)
990 PRINT USING "GROUND SPEED = ###.# MILES PER
      HOUR";SPEED
995 PRINT "TO APPLY ";GPA;" GALLONS PER ACRE"
1000 END
```

Lines 910–940 ask the user for the information needed by the program. Line 980 calculates the travel speed, and line 985 prints the results. The results would be printed in the form

```
SPEED =   4.25 MILES PER HOUR
TO APPLY 15 GALLONS PER ACRE
```

The "###.#" in line 990 controls the form in which the answer is printed. It means print the variable SPEED with three significant digits to the left of the decimal point and two significant digits to the right of the decimal. The fractional part of the answer will be rounded to the nearest hundredth. If the value of SPEED is larger than 999.9, an error will occur when the computer tries to print.

In the metric measurement system, the width would be measured in meters, the flow in liters per minute, the application rate in liters per hectare, and the speed in kilometers per hour. The program shown in Chemical Listing 2 is the metric equivalent of the previous one.

Chemical Listing 2 • Program to Calculate Sprayer Travel Speed in
Kilometers per Hour

```
890 '        GROUND SPEED CALCULATION - METRIC UNITS
900 CLS
910 INPUT "NUMBER OF NOZZLES ";NUM
920 INPUT "TOTAL SPRAY WIDTH (METERS) OF BOOM ";WIDTH
930 INPUT "FLOW RATE (LITERS/MIN) OF SINGLE NOZZLE ";
    FLOW
940 INPUT "LITERS PER HECTARE OF MATERIAL TO APPLY ";LPH
950 PRINT
980 SPEED = (10*NUM*FLOW*60.)/(WIDTH*LPH)
990 PRINT USING "SPEED = ###.# KILOMETERS PER HOUR";SPEED
995 PRINT "TO APPLY ";LPH;" LITERS PER HECTARE"
1000 END
```

The answer to Chemical Listing 2 would be in the form

```
SPEED = 8.62 KILOMETERS PER HOUR
TO APPLY 16.1 LITERS PER HECTARE
```

There are some physical restraints upon the ground speed and pumping pressure for controlling the chemical application rate. A slow ground speed will decrease the field capacity, and spraying will take too long. If the sprayer is driven too fast, it becomes difficult to operate, the equipment may be damaged, or the pumping capacity may be exceeded. The range of acceptable pumping pressures has both an upper and a lower limit. The sprayer pump may not be able to accurately maintain very low pressures. The upper pressure limit is determined by the type of pump, the power available to drive the pump, and the degree of spray droplet atomization that is acceptable.

As the pressure increases, the volume of material discharged per unit time increases, and the mean droplet size decreases. The higher the pressure, the smaller the drops. As the droplet size decreases, the material remains in the air longer. The longer the chemical remains suspended in the air, the more susceptible it is to drift. Drift means the pesticide ends up somewhere other than its intended target. Also, a longer settling time will increase the amount of evaporation.

If the droplets are too large, they may not penetrate the plant canopy and reach the underside of the plant leaves, so the insecticide being sprayed would not be as effective. Insects will actually walk around large droplets of insecticide. Small droplets are more important with pesticides than with herbicides. Droplet size can be increased either by lowering the pressure or by using a larger orifice nozzle. (The optimal droplet size for various situations is still being researched.)

If two nozzles used with the same chemical are operating at the same pressure, the one with the larger orifice will have the greater flow rate. If two identical nozzles are operated at different pressures, the one operating at the higher pressure will have the greater flow rate. When the application rate cannot be controlled by adjusting the ground speed or the pumping pressure, one must switch to a different size of spray nozzle. Nozzles are manufactured in several orifice sizes, and literature is available from the manufacturers which rates the nozzle delivery in gallons per minute at specified pressures.

Nozzle Capacity Selection

A program can be written to calculate the proper delivery rate for any particular situation. However, you must evaluate the usefulness of the answers in light of the previous discussion. The program does not take into account the affects of changing the droplet sizes with changing pressures. Neither does it place any limits on the flow rates due to physical limitations of the equipment. The user must make these decisions.

This is a good illustration of both the usefulness and the limitations of computers. The computer can manipulate information well and can quickly produce its answers. However, the computer cannot make value judgments well. In the previously mentioned situation, the program cannot evaluate the change in efficacy of the material with changes in droplet size. Nor could it decide if a particular speed was too fast for the equipment or its operator.

Never regard the computer as something to make decisions for you. Rather, view it as a tool to provide you with information on which to base your own decisions.

From the preceding section we know that the flow rate divided by the theoretical field capacity is equal to the application rate. We also know that the total flow rate for a sprayer in gallons per hour is equal to the single nozzle flow rate in gallons per minute times 60 times the number of nozzles on the spray boom. Rearranging the application rate equation to solve for the nozzle flow rate results in the equation

$$\text{FLOW} = (\text{GPA} * \text{S} * \text{W})/(8.25 * 60 * \text{N})$$

Based upon this equation one can write a program to calculate the nozzle flow rate (see Chemical Listing 3).

Chemical Listing 3 • Program to Calculate Spray Nozzle Capacity in Gallons per Minute

```
1195 '       NOZZLE CAPACITY SELECTION - GALLONS/MINUTE
1196 CLS
1200 PRINT TAB(15);"*** NOZZLE CAPACITY SELECTION ***"
1205 PRINT
1210 INPUT "NUMBER OF NOZZLES ";NUM
1220 INPUT "SPRAY WIDTH (FEET) OF BOOM ";WIDTH
1230 INPUT "GROUND SPEED (MPH) OF SPRAYER ";SPEED
1240 INPUT "APPLICATION RATE (GAL/ACRE) ";GPA
1245 '       GPM/NOZZLE = (ACRES/HOUR)*(GALLONS/ACRE)/(NO. OF
     NOZZLES*60 MIN./HR.)
1250 GM = (GPA*SPEED*WIDTH)/(8.25*60*NUM)
1255 PRINT
1260 PRINT USING "USE A NOZZLE WITH A CAPACITY OF
     ###.## GALLONS PER MINUTE AT THE RATED PRESSURE";GM
1270 END
```

The answer to Chemical Listing 3 would be printed in the form

USE A NOZZLE WITH A CAPACITY OF 1.15 GALLONS PER MINUTE AT THE RATED PRESSURE

The program shown in Chemical Listing 4 will perform the same function for nozzles rated in liters per minute.

Chemical Listing 4 • Program to Calculate Spray Nozzle Capacity in Liters per Minute

```
1195 '       NOZZLE CAPACITY SELECTION - LITERS PER MINUTE
1196 CLS
1200 PRINT TAB(15);"*** NOZZLE CAPACITY SELECTION ***"
1210 INPUT "NUMBER OF NOZZLES ";NUM
1220 INPUT "SPRAY WIDTH (METERS) ";WIDTH
1230 INPUT "GROUND SPEED (KM/HR) ";SPEED
1240 INPUT "APPLICATION RATE (LITERS/HECTARE) ";LPH
1250 LM=(LPH*SPEED*WIDTH)/(10*60*NUM)
1260 PRINT USING "USE A NOZZLE WITH A CAPACITY OF
     ###.## LITERS PER MINUTE AT THE RATED PRESSURE";LM
```

The answer to Chemical Listing 4 would be printed in the form

USE A NOZZLE WITH A CAPACITY OF 122.37 LITERS PER MINUTE AT
THE RATED PRESSURE

Sprayer Calibration

A pull-type or tractor-mounted sprayer can be calibrated when it is stationary by measuring the volume of material discharged in a measured period. To convert the results to the application rate in gallons per acre, the sprayer travel speed and spray width also need to be known. If the measured volume, V, is in fluid ounces and the time, T, is in seconds, the flow rate in gallons per hour is equal to (V/128)/(T*3600). The application rate in gallons per acre is the flow rate (gallons per hour) divided by the TFC (acres per hour).

A BASIC program for calculating a stationary sprayer is shown in Chemical Listing 5.

Chemical Listing 5 • Calibration Program for a Stationary Sprayer

```
195 '       CALIBRATION WITH STATIONARY SPRAYER - GAL/ACRE
200 INPUT "VOLUME OF CHEMICAL (FL. OZ.) ";VOL
210 INPUT "ELAPSED TIME (SECONDS) ";TIME
220 INPUT "SPEED (MPH) ";SPEED
230 INPUT "SPRAY WIDTH (FEET) ";WIDTH
240 APRATE = (VOL/128)/(TIME*3600)/(SPEED*WIDTH/8.25)
250 PRINT USING "SPRAYER APPLICATION RATE = ##.## GALLONS
    PER ACRE";APRATE
```

An alternate way of calibrating a sprayer is by driving the rig over a measured distance and measuring the amount of material applied. In this condition, the application rate in gallons per acre is given by the relationship application rate = volume applied/area covered:

$$GPA = (VOL/128)/(DIST*WIDTH/43560)$$

where

      GPA = gallons per acre
      VOL = volume of material collected, fluid ounces
     DIST = distance traveled, feet
   WIDTH = spray width, feet
   1 acre = 43,560 square feet

The program for this is shown in Chemical Listing 6.

Chemical Listing 6 • Calibration Program for a Moving Sprayer

```
190 'CALIBRATION WITH MOVING SPRAYER - GALLONS/ACRE
195 '
200 INPUT "VOLUME (FL. OZ.) ";VOL
210 INPUT "DISTANCE TRAVELED (FT) ";DIST
220 INPUT "SPRAY WIDTH (FT) ";WIDTH
230 GPA = (VOL/128)/(DIST*WIDTH/43560)
240 PRINT "APPLICATION RATE ";GPA;" GALLONS PER ACRE"
```

Chemical Mixing Ratios

Pesticides and other materials are usually mixed with water and applied as an aqueous solution. The materials may come as wettable powders or liquids. A proper mixing ratio is essential for applying the material at the correct rate.

Wettable powders

Application rates for powders are specified in pounds per acre (or kilograms per hectare). To determine the amount of powder to mix with a spray tank, one must know 1) the desired application rate for the powder, 2) the sprayer flow rate, and 3) the volume of the spray tank. The total amount of powder per tank will be equal to the number of pounds of powder per acre multiplied by the number of acres that can be covered with one tank full of solution. The number of acres per tank is equal to the volume of the tank divided by the solution application rate. Expressed as an equation, the application rate for powdered chemicals would be

pounds powder/tank = (# pounds powder/acre)*(acres/tank)

Liquid chemicals

The application rate is similar for liquids, except that the volume of the chemicals must be accounted for when filling the tank. That is, one would need to place the chemicals in the tank before completely filling it with water. Expressed as an equation, the application rate for liquid chemicals would be

gal. chemical/tank = (gal. chemical/acre)*(acres/tank)

Mixing two or more chemicals

At times it might be advantageous to combine two or three chemicals and apply them together. To do this, one would calculate the mixing ratios for each chemical separately, then add their separate amounts to the tank, and finally fill the rest of the tank with water.

The BASIC program shown in Chemical Listing 7 will calculate mixing ratios for one to three chemicals by weight or volume.

Chemical Listing 7 • Chemical Mixing Ratio Program for Sprayers

```
  1 '       CHEMICAL MIXING RATIOS
400 CLS:PRINT TAB(15);"*** CHEMICAL MIXING RATIOS ***":PRINT
410 PRINT "THIS PROGRAM CAN BE USED TO CALCULATE THE MIXING
      AMOUNTS FOR "
415 PRINT "1 TO 3 CHEMICALS MIXED TOGETHER WITH WATER (OR
      OTHER SPRAY MEDIUM)"
420 PRINT:PRINT "THE APPLICATION RATE FOR EACH OF THE
      CHEMICALS CAN BE"
425 PRINT "SPECIFIED IN PINTS, GALLONS, OR POUNDS PER ACRE":
      PRINT
430 PRINT "THE APPLICATION RATE FOR THE SPRAYER MUST BE IN
      GALLONS PER ACRE"
435 PRINT:INPUT "PRESS <ENTER> KEY TO CONTINUE ";A$
436 ' ---------------------------------------------------
437 '       ENTER CHEMICAL NAMES, AMOUNTS, AND UNITS
438 '
440 CLS:INPUT "ENTER THE NUMBER OF CHEMICALS TO MIX ";N%
445 IF (N%<1) OR (N%>3) THEN 440
450 DIM CHEM$(N%),UNIT%(N%),AMT(N%),RATE(N%),UNIT$(3)
455 PRINT
457 UNIT$(1)=" PINTS"
458 UNIT$(2)=" GALLONS"
459 UNIT$(3)=" POUNDS"
460 FOR I=1 TO N%
465 PRINT "ENTER NAME OF CHEMICAL NUMBER ";I;
470 INPUT CHEM$(I):PRINT
475 PRINT "1 - ";UNIT$(1)
476 PRINT "2 - ";UNIT$(2)
477 PRINT "3 - ";UNIT$(3)
480 PRINT:PRINT "ENTER NUMBER CORRESPONDING TO UNITS FOR ";
      CHEM$(I);
485 INPUT UNIT%(I)
486 IF (UNIT%(I)<1) OR (UNIT%(I)>3) THEN PRINT
      "*** INVALID ENTRY - PLEASE TRY AGAIN ***":GOTO 465
490 PRINT "ENTER APPLICATION RATE - ";UNIT$(UNIT%(I));" PER
      ACRE FOR ";CHEM$(I)
495 INPUT RATE(I):PRINT
500 NEXT I
505 INPUT "ENTER SPRAY TANK SIZE (GALLONS) ";GAL:PRINT
```

```
510 INPUT "ENTER TOTAL SPRAYING RATE (GALLONS PER ACRE)
    ";SPRAY:PRINT
520 ' ------------------------------------------------
521 '        CALCULATE MIXING RATIOS
530 ACRES = GAL/SPRAY        'ACRES COVERED PER TANK
540 CVOL = 0         'CVOL IS TOTAL VOLUME OF CHEMICAL PER TANK
    OF SPRAY
550 FOR I=1 TO N%
555 AMT(I)=RATE(I)*ACRES
560 ON UNIT%(I) GOTO 570,580,590
570 CVOL=CVOL+AMT(I)
575 GOTO 590
580 CVOL=CVOL+AMT(I)/8
590 NEXT I
600 ' ------------------------------------------------
602 '        PRINT RESULTS
610 CLS
611 PRINT STRING$(60,"-")
615 PRINT "CHEMICAL";TAB(25);"APPLICATION RATE"
620 FOR I=1 TO N%
630 PRINT CHEM$(I);TAB(25);RATE(I);UNIT$(UNIT%(I));" PER
    ACRE"
640 NEXT I
650 PRINT:PRINT GAL;" GALLON SPRAYER":PRINT
660 PRINT SPRAY;" GALLONS PER ACRE SPRAY RATE":PRINT
665 PRINT STRING$(60,"-"):PRINT
670 PRINT TAB(15);"CHEMICAL MIXING RATIOS":PRINT
680 PRINT "CHEMICAL";TAB(30);"ADD"
685 '        PRINT CHEMICAL NAMES AND AMOUNT TO ADD PER TANK
690 FOR I=1 TO N%
700 PRINT CHEM$(I);TAB(25);
705 PRINT USING "####.#";AMT(I);:PRINT UNIT$(UNIT%(I));" PER
    TANK"
710 NEXT I
720 PRINT "WATER";TAB(25);
721 '  GAL-CVOL IS TANK CAPACITY MINUS VOLUME OF CHEMICALS
722 PRINT USING "####.# GALLONS PER TANK";GAL-CVOL
725 PRINT:PRINT STRING$(60,"-")
730 END
```

Discussion of chemical mixing ratio program

The mixing program in Chemical Listing 7 uses the English measurement system. A program with metric units would be very similar.

Instructions for using the program are printed on the screen to inform the user of the allowable units. The name of each chemical is entered into the computer and included in the results to avoid confusion. The units are printed for each chemical in the results for the same reason.

When calculating the amount of water that must be added to the chemicals to fill the tank, the volumes of the liquid are subtracted from the tank's capacity, but the volume of the powders is ignored.

Chemical Application by Aircraft

Although no program listing is included for chemical application by aircraft, the subject is discussed here to give the reader another microcomputer application.

Discussion of aerial application

When chemicals are applied to a field with a ground-driven rig, they are usually transported to the field either in a nurse tank or truck, and the sprayer is refilled in the field. The shape of the field is not too important with respect to field efficiency, since a relatively small amount of the total time is spent in making the turns.

With aerial application by fixed-wing aircraft, the situation is quite different. The chemicals are stored either at the home base or at a remote landing strip. The pilot must return to the base or landing strip each time he or she refills the plane's tank. The time to spray a field by air is very dependent upon the shape of the field. The best shape from the standpoint of the applicator is a long, narrow field with no obstructions. Extra time is consumed and wasted each time the plane has to make a turn at the end of a field. Turning time becomes a very significant part of the application time. When the costs of running a plane may be a few hundred dollars per hour, both the shuttle time (time spent flying between the landing strip and the field where the chemical is applied) and the turnaround time at the end of swaths become very costly.

Most applicators charge a flat fee per acre for spraying, based upon the chemicals used, the rate of application, and perhaps the total number of acres sprayed. However, the applicator's operating costs are affected by the previously mentioned factors of distance from base and field shape. A computer program could help applicators determine their actual costs under various operating conditions, and possibly let them charge lower rates for nearby, well-shaped fields, and at the same time ensure they cover their costs in less desirable situations. Of course, there are other factors that cannot be programmed which would affect their final pricing structure, such as the kind of competition and customer relations. Remember, the computer can only compare alternatives that can be expressed in mathematical terms.

Developing an aerial application costs program

The objective of an aerial application costs program would be to determine the total costs for applying chemicals to a particular site. The answer would probably be expressed in dollars per acre (or hectare). The total costs would have to include both the fixed costs (those costs independent of the amount of time the aircraft is used) and the variable costs (those costs dependent upon the amount of usage).

Fixed costs. The fixed costs would be the same as discussed in other sections in this book: depreciation, interest on investment, insurance, housing, etc.

Variable costs. Pilot wages would be considered a variable cost if the pilot was paid by the number of hours he or she flew. If the pilot was salaried, the wages would be a fixed cost. Repair, maintenance, inspections, and overhauls would be variable costs, as would fuel and lubrication. The cost of the chemicals themselves would be another variable expense.

A computer program would be very useful in calculating the operator's application costs, particularly if the costs were different for each field and with each chemical applied. Because others have already realized this, some programs have been developed for both microcomputers and programmable calculators. If you are interested in one of them, be certain you consider all of the factors that affect your particular cost structure.

Summary

Chemicals are an integral part of agricultural production in many areas of the world. Some programs have been presented in this chapter that can help the farmer reduce application errors. It would not take too many mistakes in application rates on a large farm to justify a computer for this one task alone.

We may not be too far from the day when we will see the farmer tell the computer the crop and soil conditions and have it respond with a list of which chemicals to apply, the rate at which they should be applied, and when they should be applied. Some day the computer may serve as a diagnostician, recommending chemicals to solve some of the production problems that producers must face.

Chapter 10
Greenhouses and nurseries

This chapter on greenhouses and nurseries has just one computer program in it. The program is different from the ones in the previous chapters because it includes disk operations. Disk operations were not included earlier because of the many variations in commands with the different disk operating systems used by the various microcomputers. They are included here to give you an appreciation for the complexity added to a program when disk input/output becomes necessary. The program was written specifically to run on a Radio Shack® Model II Microcomputer™ using a Microsoft®* BASIC interpreter. Some of the disk commands may have to be modified for the program to work on other computers.

The microcomputer can perform many roles in the greenhouse and plant nursery. It can maintain inventories, print letters and reports, and handle financial and personnel records. The computer can schedule operations, turn sprinklers on and off, control temperatures and humidity, and notify an operator when something is wrong with the equipment.

A business dealing with live plants needs a way to quickly and easily monitor and control its inventory. The manager might need information such as the sales patterns of plants and other materials. An inventory program could schedule ordering times of new materials based upon the present stock level and the ordering and restocking time. For instance, if six widgets are used every week and it takes four weeks to get more widgets after an order has been placed, the computer could notify the operator when the stock of widgets is down to 24 and prepare a purchase order. While these tasks could be handled manually, they may be worth computerizing when the inventory becomes very complex or the cost of not having an item when needed is very high. A hardware store or parts department in a farm implement dealer are some other businesses where an inventory monitoring and automatic reordering scheme could be cost-effective.

Using a microcomputer for monitoring and controlling a greenhouse environment requires a working knowledge of transducers and analog electronics. These subjects are too broad to address in this book. Environmental control systems do not require a knowledge of electronics to use and can be purchased to handle the situation. Commercial programs are available to handle bookkeeping, word processing, and financial records with small computers. This chapter concentrates on the function of creating and maintaining records for plant operations.

---

*Microsoft® is a registered trademark of Microsoft Corporation.

The Cultural Schedule Record

The cultural schedule record is a record of all operations or activities to perform on a crop. Table 10-1, from Paul Nelson's book *Greenhouse Operation and Management,* shows a typical cultural schedule record for use in a greenhouse. It contains a list of all operations, the scheduled performance date, the completion date, the person performing the operation, and a section for manager certification. There is also a section for the crop or plant description and its location.

A greenhouse might contain several lists such as the one shown in Table 10-1 for different sets of plants or crops. In the example, several lots of mums could be planted on different dates. Each set could need the same operations performed at identical times in the plant's life cycle. For example, pruning plants back to two or three shoots might always occur 43 days after planting. The problem is all of the scheduled dates have to

TABLE 10-1 • A Typical Cultural Schedule Record

Greenhouse		Benches	Crop	Cultivar	
[IV]		[9-15]	[Cut Mums]	[Nob Hill]	
Date scheduled	Date accomplished	Operation		Empl.	Mgr. Initials
3-7-78		Plant 7″ × 8″			
3-7		Fertilize, half strength			
3-7		Start lighting at night			
3-14		Fertilize and spray			
3-21		Fertilize and spray			
3-28		Pinch			
3-28		Fertilize and spray			
4-4		Fertilize and spray			
4-11		Fertilize and spray			
. . .					
. . .					
. . .					
6-24		Harvest			

Note: Reprinted by permission, from *Greenhouse Operation and Management* by Paul V. Nelson, Reston Publishing Co., Inc., Reston, VA, 1982.

be refigured every time the scheduled date of the first operation is changed.

When calculating the operation dates by hand, it is easy to make numerical errors. The computer can eliminate these errors. A method is needed to (1) create and save cultural records and (2) schedule the dates for all plant activities, based upon the date of the first operation (planting date). The method should allow for several types of operations for different crops. Ideally, these schedules could be stored and recalled as needed so any one kind of schedule need only be created once. For example, if different varieties of roses required special treatment, a separate schedule of operations could be provided for each one. The user could recall the cultural schedule form for the XYZ rose, enter the scheduled date of the first task, and receive a printout of the complete record with all the calendar dates for succeeding operations.

The cultural schedule should satisfy two objectives:

1. It should be able to create and store cultural schedule record forms with any number and type of operations.

2. It should be able to print a complete record with all scheduled dates based on the date of the first operation.

The computer program can be developed in two main sections. One section will create new cultural schedules and store them on the disk. Included in this section will be a method for modifying an existing schedule. (It is always good to allow for changes.) The second section will print any given selected schedule with the scheduled dates for all operations.

Before the program is listed, a few comments need to be made about the disk operating system commands that appear in the listing. The line numbers in parentheses refer to a place in the program where that particular command is used.

OPEN (Line 1000) • The OPEN "D",1,"CULTURE/DIR",55 command opens a direct-access file ("D") for reading and writing by the computer program. The name of the file is CULTURE/DIR, and each record in it is 55 characters long. The numeral 1 informs the operating system that whenever a FIELD, PUT, GET, or LOF statement use file number 1, they are referring to the CULTURE/DIR file. Record lengths in direct-access files must all be the same, and the computer must be told the length for it to properly access the records in any specified order. If the specified file name already existed when the OPEN command was given, it would be opened. If it did not previously exist, the OPEN command would create it.

FIELD (Line 1005) • The FIELD 1,6 as FILNAM$,49 AS DESC$ command designates how the records in file 1 are divided into fields. This record has two fields: the first one, FILNAM$, is 6 characters long, and the second one, DESC$, is 49 characters long. The total length of all of the fields must be equal to the record length.

LOF(1) (Line 1012) • LOF(1) is a length-of-file function, which contains the number of records in the opened file specified by the number in parentheses. If LOF(1) was zero, that would mean the file was a new one and did not contain any information.

LSET (Line 2030) • LSET places a string in a field of a direct access record. If the string is shorter than the number of characters specified in the FIELD statement, it is placed in the left part of the field, and the rest is filled with blanks. If the string is longer than the field, the rightmost characters of the string are truncated (chopped off) so the string will not overflow the field.

PUT (Line 2030) • PUT 1 puts the record defined by the LSET statements into file number 1 immediately following the last previous record in the file.

MKS$ (Line 2230) • MKS$ converts a single-precision numeric to its corresponding string value. Only string values can be stored in direct access files. There are other forms similar to MKS$ for converting integers and double-precision numbers to strings.

GET (Line 3670) • GET 1,I gets the record number I and places it in the variables defined by the FIELD statement. In this program, the GET statement would place the leftmost 4 characters of record number I into the variable DAY$ (Line 3620) and the other 51 characters into DESC$.

CLOSE (Line 3700) • Close 1 closes file number 1 to prevent any further access to it until it is reopened by an OPEN statement.

BASIC Listing for Cultural Schedule Program

```
1 'CULTURAL SCHEDULE RECORDS PROGRAM
5 CLEAR 5000 : CLS
6 PRINT TAB(10);"CREATE/PRINT CULTURAL SCHEDULE RECORDS":
  PRINT
7 PRINT "CALCULATES CALENDAR DATE OF ALL OPERATIONS BASED
  UPON THE DATE OF THE FIRST OPERATION"
9 FULL = 22       '22 LINES ALLOWED ON SCREEN
10 PRINT
12 ' ----------------------------------------------------
13 '       FUNCTIONS FOR DATE CONVERSIONS
15 DEFFNDV%(A1$,A2%) = (VAL(A1$)>0) AND (VAL(A1$)<13) AND
   (VAL(MID$(A1$,4))>0) AND (VAL(MID$(A1$,4))<32) AND
   (VAL(MID$(A1$,7))>=A2%) AND (LEN(A1$) = 10)

51 DEFFNDN!(Y%,M%,D%) = Y%*365+INT((Y%-1)/4)+(M%-1)*28 +
   VAL(MID$("00030306081131619212426",(M%-1)*2+1,2)) -
   ((M%>2) AND ((Y%ANDNOT-4)=0))+D%
```

```
 52 DEFFNRY%(N!)=INT((N!-N!/1461)/365)
 53 DEFFNRJ%(N!)=N!-(FNRY%(N!)*365+INT((FNRY%(N!)-1)/4))
 54 DEFFNRM%(J%,Y%)=-((Y%ANDNOT-4)<>0)*(1- (J%>31)-
    (J%>59)-
    (J%>90)-(J%>120)-(J%>151)-(J%>181)-(J%>212)-(J%>243)-
    (J%>273)-(J%>304)-(J%>334))-((Y%ANDNOT-4)=0)*
    (1-(J%>31)-(J%>60)-(J%>91)-(J%>121)-(J%>152)-(J%>182)-
    (J%>213)-(J%>244)-(J%>274)-(J%>305)-(J%>335))
 55 DEFFNRD%(Y%,M%,J%)=(J%-((M%-1)*28+
    VAL(MID$("000303060811131619212426",(M%-1)*2+1,2))))+
    ((M%>2) AND((Y%ANDNOT-4)=0))
100 ' ----------------------------------------------------
104 '          PRINT MENU
105 PRINT TAB(10);"CULTURAL SCHEDULE PROGRAM" : PRINT
110 PRINT TAB(38):"MENU":PRINT"ITEM";TAB(15);"DESCRIPTION"
120 PRINT "1";TAB(10);"CREATE NEW CULTURAL SCHEDULE"
130 PRINT "2";TAB(10);"PRINT CULTURAL SCHEDULE RECORD WITH
    CALENDAR DATES"
140 PRINT "3";TAB(10);"PRINT CULTURAL SCHEDULE
    WITH RELATIVE DATES"
145 PRINT "4";TAB(10);"LIST DIRECTORY OF CULTURAL SCHEDULE
    RECORDS ON PRINTER"
150 PRINT "5";TAB(10);"MODIFY EXISTING CULTURAL SCHEDULE"
160 PRINT "6";TAB(10);"QUIT"
190 PRINT:INPUT "SELECT ITEM NUMBER AND PRESS <ENTER> ";N
200 ON N GOTO 2000,3000,3500,4000,5000,210
210 END
985 ' ----------------------------------------------------
995 '        DIRECTORY LISTING
1000 OPEN "D",1,"CULTURE/DIR",55
1005 FIELD 1,6 AS FILNAM$,49 AS DESC$
1010 CLS:PRINT TAB(5);"EXISTING CULTURAL SCHEDULES":PRINT
1011 COUNT=1:NUM = LOF(1)
1012 DIM DIRECT$(LOF(1),2)   'ARRAY FOR NAMES & DESCRIPTIONS
1013 IF LOF(1)=0 THEN PRINT "NO EXISTING CULTURAL
     SCHEDULES" : PRINT : RETURN
1014 PRINT "FILE        DESCRIPTION":PRINT"NAME":PRINT
1015 FOR I=1 TO LOF(1)
1020 GET 1
1021 DIRECT$(I,1)=FILNAM$
1022 DIRECT$(I,2)=DESC$
1025 PRINT FILNAM$;TAB(10);DESC$
1030 COUNT=COUNT+1 : IF COUNT=FULL THEN GOSUB
     10000 'PAUSE
     IF SCREEN IS FULL
1035 NEXT I
1040 RETURN
1100 ' ----------------------------------------------------
1999 '             CREATE NEW CULTURAL SCHEDULE
2000 GOSUB 1000 'PRINT EXISTING SCHEDULES FIRST
2005 ERASE DIRECT$   'DELETE ARRAY TO ALLOW FOR LATER
     EXPANSION
```

```
2010 PRINT
2015 PRINT "ENTER (UNIQUE) NAME FOR NEW CULTURAL SCHEDULE
     - UP TO 6 CHARACTERS" : INPUT "(OR Q TO QUIT) ";NAM$
2020 IF LEFT$(NAM$,1)="Q" THEN CLOSE 1 : GOTO 105
2025 PRINT "ENTER DESCRIPTION OF FILE - UP TO 49
     CHARACTERS " : INPUT D$
2030 LSET FILNAM$=NAM$:LSET DESC$=D$:PUT 1:CLOSE 1
2035 '
2040 '      THE NEW NAME IS NOW ADDED TO THE DIRECTORY
2045 '      BEGIN CREATING THE NEW CULTURAL SCHEDULE
2060 DIM D(50),D$(50)        'UP TO 50 OPERATIONS ALLOWED -
     CAN BE CHANGED IF NEEDED
2062 CLS : PRINT NAM$;" CULTURAL SCHEDULE"
2063 PRINT:PRINT "DAYS IS NUMBER OF DAYS AFTER FIRST
     OPERATION"
2064 PRINT "E.G., IF 2ND OPERATION IS ON SAME DAY AS FIRST
     OPERATION, ENTER 0"
2065 PRINT"ENTER 1 IF THE OPERATION IS ON THE NEXT DAY,
     ETC."
2066 PRINT "ENTER A NEGATIVE NUMBER FOR DAY NUMBER WHEN
     FINISHED":PRINT
2068 PRINT "OPER";TAB(8);"DAYS";TAB(15);"OPERATION" :
     PRINT" NO."
2070 X=10
2071 FOR OP=1 TO 50
2075 PRINT@(X,0),OP; : IF OP=1 THEN PRINT@(X,9),"0":D=0:
     GOTO 2085
2080 PRINT@(X,7),; : INPUT D(OP): IF D(OP)<0 THEN NUM =
     OP−1:GOTO 2210
2085 PRINT@(X,14),; : INPUT D$(OP)
2100 X=X+1:GOSUB 2950
2105 IF X=26 THEN GOSUB 2960   'REACHED END OF SCREEN ===>
     CLEAR SCREEN
2110 NEXT OP
2200 IF NUM<1 THEN N=50:PRINT"MAXIMUM NUMBER OF
     OPERATIONSEXCEEDED"
2205 PRINT "FIRST 50 ARE BEING STORED"
2210 OPEN "D",1,NAM$,55
2215 FIELD 1,4 AS DAY$,51 AS DESC$
2220 PRINT:PRINT "STORING CULTURAL RECORD UNDER FILE NAME ";
     NAM$
2225 FOR I=1 TO NUM
2230 LSET DAY$=MKS$(D(I)):LSET DESC$=D$(I)
2240 PUT 1
2250 NEXT I
2260 CLOSE 1
2270 RUN        'RETURN TO MAIN MENU
2949 '      UPDATE LENGTH OF FILE COUNT
2950 PRINT@(0,35),USING"### OPERATIONS";OP:RETURN
2959 '      CLEAR DATA AREA OF SCREEN
2960 X=10:PRINT@(10,0),"";:FOR I=10 to 22 : PRINT STRING$(79,"") :
     NEXT I :RETURN
2998 ' ------------------------------------------------------
```

```
2999 '        PRINT CULTURAL SCHEDULE RECORD WITH DATES
3000 GOSUB 1000 : CLOSE 1
3001 CLS:PRINT "PRINT CULTURAL SCHEDULE RECORD WITH DATES" :
     PRINT
3005 INPUT "ENTER NAME OF CULTURAL SCHEDULE FILE ";FILNAM$
3008 PRINT: INPUT "ENTER CULTIVAR DESCRIPTION ";CD$
3009 PRINT:INPUT "ENTER LOCATION OF BOX OR FLAT ";BL$
3010 OPEN "D",1,FILNAM$,55
3015 FIELD 1,4 AS DAY$,51 AS DESC$
3016 '        CHECK FOR EMPTY FILE
3017 IF LOF(1)=0 THEN CLOSE 1:KILL FILNAM$:PRINT "***";
     FILNAM$;" DOES NOT EXIST ***":GOTO 3005
3020 INPUT "ENTER DATE OF FIRST OPERATION IN THE FORM -
     MM/DD/YYYY ";D1$
3025 IF FNDV%(D1$,1900) THEN 3026 ELSE PRINT "INVALID DATE":
     GOTO 3020
3026 M%=VAL(MID$(D1$,1)):D%=VAL(MID$(D1$,4)) :
     Y%=VAL(MID$(D1$,7))
3029 '            PRINT HEADER SECTION
3030 LPRINT TAB(20);"FILE ";FILNAM$:LPRINT
3035 LPRINT "CULTIVAR - ";CD$:LPRINT
3040 LPRINT "LOCATION - ";BL$:LPRINT
3200 FOR I=1 TO LOF(1)
3210 GET 1
3215 DT=CVS(DAY$)                'DAYS AFTER FIRST OPERATION
3220 N!=FNDN!(Y%,M%,D%)+DT
3230 Y%=FNRY%(N!)
3231 J%=FNRJ%(N!)
3232 M%=FNRM%(J%,Y%)
3233 D%=FNRD%(Y%,M%,J%)
3240 LPRINT USING "##/##/####";M%,D%,Y%;:LPRINT
     TAB(20);DESC$
3250 NEXT I
3260 CLOSE 1
3270 RUN          'RETURN TO MAIN MENU
3480 ' ------------------------------------------------
3500 GOSUB 1000   'PRINT NAMES OF EXISTING SCHEDULES
3505 CLOSE 1
3510 PRINT:PRINT "PRINT SCHEDULE WITH RELATIVE DATES"
3520 PRINT
3530 INPUT "ENTER NAME OF DESIRED CULTURAL SCHEDULE, OR Q
     TO QUIT ";F$
3531 IF (F$="Q") THEN CLOSE 1:RUN    'START OVER IF QUIT
3535 F=0
3540 FOR I=1 TO NUM
3550 IF F$=DIRECT$(I,1) THEN F=I:I=NUM   'EXIT LOOP IF
     NAME FOUND
3560 NEXT I
3565 IF F>0 THEN 3610   'F>0 ===> FILE NAME WAS FOUND
3570 PRINT:PRINT TAB(15);"*** FILE NAME NOT FOUND ***"
3580 PRINT:INPUT "PRESS <ENTER> KEY FOR A LIST OF THE
     EXISTING CULTURAL SCHEDULES ";Q$
3590 GOTO 3500
```

```
3610 OPEN "D",1,F$,55
3620 FIELD 1,4 AS DAY$,51 AS DESC$
3625 '       PRINT FILE NAME AND DESCRIPTION
3630 LPRINT DIRECT$(F,1);TAB(10); DIRECT$(F,2)
3640 LPRINT:LPRINT "DAYS AFTER";TAB(15);"OPERATION"
3650 LPRINT "1ST OPER.":LPRINT
3660 FOR I=1 TO LOF(1)
3670 GET 1,I
3680 LPRINT DAY$;TAB(10);DESC$
3690 NEXT I
3700 CLOSE 1
3710 RUN         'RETURN TO MAIN MENU
3990 ' ------------------------------------------------
3999 '       LIST CULTURAL SCHEDULES ON PRINTER
4000 OPEN "D",1,"CULTURE/DIR",55
4010 IF LOF(1)>0 THEN 4050
4020 CLOSE 1
4025 PRINT
4030 PRINT "NO RECORDS IN DIRECTORY"
4040 PRINT:GOTO 105
4045 '       PRINT RECORDS
4050 FIELD 1,6 AS FILNAM$,49 AS DESC$
4055 LPRINT "FILE NAME";TAB(20);"DESCRIPTION":LPRINT
4060 FOR I=1 TO LOF(1)
4070 GET 1
4080 LPRINT FILNAM$;TAB(20);DESC$
4090 NEXT I
4100 CLOSE 1
4110 RUN         'RETURN TO MAIN MENU
4125 ' ------------------------------------------------
4999 '              UPDATE/MODIFY EXISTING CULTURAL SCHEDULE
5000 INPUT "ENTER NAME OF CULTURAL SCHEDULE TO UPDATE OR
     MODIFY ";F$
5010 OPEN "D",1,F$,55
5030 FIELD 1,4 AS DAY$,51 AS DESC$
5040 INPUT "ENTER RECORD NUMBER TO CHANGE OR Q TO QUIT
     ";N$
5045 IF ((N$="Q")OR(N$="q")) THEN CLOSE 1:RUN
5050 GET 1,VAL(N$)
5060 PRINT DAY$;TAB(10);DESC$
5070 INPUT "ENTER NEW DAY VALUE OR Q TO QUIT ";A$
5080 IF((A$="Q")OR(A$="q")) THEN CLOSE 1 : GOTO 105
5090 LSET DAY$=MKS(VAL(A$)):PRINT
5100 INPUT "ENTER NEW DESCRIPTION ";A$
5110 LSET DESC$ = A$
5120 PUT 1,VAL(N$)
5130 GOTO 5040
9990 ' ------------------------------------------------
9995 '       PAUSE WHEN SCREEN IS FULL
10000 COUNT=1
10005 INPUT "PRESS <ENTER> TO CONTINUE ";Q$
10010 RETURN
```

Functions for date manipulations

The Listing for the Cultural Schedule Program requires several manipulations of calendar dates. The section of the program from line 13 through line 55 is a series of functions for performing various date conversions. These functions were taken from Lewis Rosenfelder's book *BASIC Faster and Better & Other Mysteries*. Rosenfelder's book contains many excellent, commonly-used routines for programming in BASIC. His use of these routines is an example of not reinventing the wheel. Whenever possible (both legally and ethically), it is best to spend programming time to develop new programs rather than redoing programs others have already written.

The functions are compact and are not easy to understand, since they were written for efficiency of operation and economy of memory. Most of the rest of the programs in this book could be condensed in a somewhat similar fashion and still accomplish their purpose, but they would be more difficult to understand. For example, all of the comments could be eliminated. This would save memory and speed up the program but would make the program more difficult to understand and to modify.

How the functions work

The reader can skip this section on how the functions work and still understand the operation of the main program. It is included for those more interested in the details of how functions work.

Function DV% (line 15) checks for a valid date function, where a valid date is defined to be of the form MM/DD/YYYY. MM is a two-digit number for the month, DD is a two-digit number for the day of the month, and YYYY is a four-digit year. The function tests if MM is strictly between 0 and 13, and if DD is strictly between 0 and 32, and if YYYY is greater than the value specified in the parameter A2%, and if the length of the character string is 10 characters including the "/" symbols.

If an integer number is strictly between 19 and 31, it can have any integer value from 20 through 30, but it cannot have the values 19 or 31. In this example, *parameter* refers to a number or variable that the function gets from the statement which called it. Suppose a function had been defined by the statement

DEF FN A(B,C) = (2*B) + (3*C).

Whenever function A is used in the program, such as

E−FN A(1,F),

the first parameter, the number 1, is used wherever B is used in the function, and the second parameter, the present value of the variable, F, would be substituted for the letter C. If F had a value of 10, E would have a value of $(2*1)+(3*10)$, or 32. Different valued parameters would result in different values being returned for the value of function A.

In the case of the date functions, the functions produce logical values—TRUE or FALSE. A logical expression of the form Y = D AND E is true if both D and E are TRUE. If either D or E or both D and E are FALSE, Y is FALSE. The logical expression Y = D OR E is TRUE if either D or E, or both E and E are TRUE. Y is FALSE only when neither D nor E are TRUE. NOT inverts the value of a logical expression or value. NOT TRUE is FALSE, and NOT FALSE is TRUE. In the function DV%, if the value of A1$ is greater and its value is less than 13, the expression (VAL(A1$)>0) AND (VAL(A1$)<13) is TRUE. Otherwise, it is FALSE.

Functions DN! (line 51), RY% (line 52), RJ% (line 53), RM% (line 54), and RD% (line 55) are used to calculate the calendar dates of the operations based upon the date of the first operation and the number of days after the first date of each operation.

Directory listing

The directory listing (lines 995–1040) allows the user to examine all of the cultural records previously created and stored on file, and gives a description of each record. The COUNT variable is used to keep track of how many lines are printed on the screen. If there were more records than lines on the screen, the records would begin scrolling off the top of the screen as more were printed at the bottom. This would make it difficult to read the information, so the program is set to pause when the screen is full. Printing continues after the <ENTER> key is pressed. The COUNT variable is then reset, and the printing continues to pause each time the screen becomes full. (If your computer produces a different number of lines on your monitor, change the value of FULL in line 9 to match your system.)

Create new cultural schedule

Lines 1999–2960 contain the information for creating a new cultural schedule. All of the cultural schedule names are kept in a directory file named "CULTURE/DIR". The LOF(1) contains the number of records in the file. If it is zero, a message is presented to inform the user that no schedule exists. When creating a new schedule, first list the existing schedules to ensure the new schedule will be assigned an unused name. In this example, names are allowed to be from 1 to 6 characters in length, although the system actually allows 7 character names followed by a "/" and up to three more characters. The length and form of acceptable file names must be compatible with your computer. Otherwise, when the system tries to open a file with that name, an error will occur and the program will stop running. Also change the instructions that explain the allowable file names.

After the name and description of the new cultural schedule are specified, they are entered into the cultural schedule directory. In its present form, the program does not check for duplicate file names. If this feature is desired, insert the following lines into the program.

```
2021 FOR J=1 TO LOF(1)
2022 GET 1,J
2023 IF NAM$=FILNAM$ THEN PRINT "FILE ALREADY EXISTS"
2024 NEXT J
```

In line 2060, variables D and D$ are dimensioned to 50. Actually, in the version of BASIC on the TRS 80 Model II and in some other versions, the DIM statement dimensions the variables to 51 elements because D(0) and D$(0) are included. These zero elements are generally ignored in this book since I believe it is less confusing to begin with element number 1 instead of 0. If memory space was critical, the zero elements would need to be used. If space is not at a premium, it is better to strive for clarity of programming rather than conservation of space.

The size of the arrays D and D$ set a maximum limit of 50 on how many operations can be included in one cultural record. There are two ways of increasing this limit. One way is to increase the size of the arrays with the DIM statement. The second way is to use simple, undimensioned variables and put the information on the disk after each operation is entered.

The advantage of this second method is there is no limit to the number of operations except the storage capacity of the data disk. The disadvantage is the large number of disk input/output operations that are required. Storing an entire array at one time causes less wear on the disk drive, and is quicker because fewer disk accesses are required. A dimensioned array was used in this program because of the disadvantage just mentioned.

Lines 2062–2068 identify the file name of the cultural record and give instructions for entering the data. The instructions should remain on the screen all the time so the operator will not have to memorize them (what if he forgets how to quit?). If they do not, the operator should be able to recall the instructions when creating the cultural record. Since the instructions here are only a few lines, they can remain on the screen. If they were longer, an alternative means of accessing them would have to be provided. One alternative would be to allow the word "HELP" to be typed in for the operation description. Another way would be to allow a specific negative number, such as −1, to be entered in the number of days entry. The input routines for entering "HELP" as the operation description could take the form of the following:

IF D$(I) = "HELP" THEN GOSUB HELP

where the variable HELP is the line number of a subroutine that would print the instructions. If the HELP subroutine was called by entering −1 for the number of days, one could use the statement

IF D(I) = −1 THEN GOSUB HELP

Line 2960 is used to clear the screen area reserved for entering the data after the screen becomes full. By clearing only the data entry area, the instructions remain on the screen. It uses a PRINT@(X,Y) form of the PRINT statement. PRINT@(X,Y) causes the information to be printed in line X and column Y on the screen. On the machine used in writing this program, there were 80 columns and 24 lines.

Print cultural schedule record

The printing section (lines 2999–3260) requires the operator to identify the file name, the calendar date of the first operation, and some title information. The title information should be tailored to fit the particular needs of the user. In the example program, the user is asked to enter the cultivar and its location (lines 3008–3009). After the file name, cultivar, and location are printed, the cultural schedule record is printed with all of the operations and their actual completion dates.

Lines 3220 through 3233 convert the number of days following the first operation to the corresponding date by using the functions DN!, RY%, RJ%, RM% and RD%. Line 3240 prints the date in a MM/DD/YYYY format, which is followed by a description of the operation to be performed.

If your particular business is very complex, it may be desirable to add another feature at this point in the program. One could store the information on disk as well as make a copy on the line printer. If this was done, the computer could provide daily or weekly listings of the greenhouse operations to be performed on any of the groups of plants and the location of the groups.

To accomplish this, the calendar date, operation, cultivar, and its location would have to be stored for each operation. That would require a large amount of disk space and probably would not be desirable except in very large operations. It might be easier to make an extra copy of each printout and examine them manually to schedule the operations for each worker.

Print schedule with relative dates

Lines 3500–3700 allow the user to check a cultural schedule for the correct form and number of days for each entry. Once a valid file name is found, all of its records are read and printed on the line printer.

List schedule directory on line printer

Lines 4000–4100 send a listing of all of the cultural schedules which have been already defined to the line printer. The CULTURE/DIR file is opened, read, printed, and closed.

Modify existing cultural schedule

The last section of the program (lines 5000–5120) has been included to allow one to make changes in existing schedules. A change might be necessary if a mistake was made in the original schedule or if some operational changes had occurred. The section asks for the file name and the specific record number that needs to be changed. The requested record is printed, and the user is allowed to make any desired changes. After the changes are made, the disk file is updated, and the user is prompted for more changes or to stop.

Summary

The greenhouse and nursery operation offers many interesting applications for microcomputer systems. For example, the systems can be used for environmental control, work scheduling, and inventory control. A computerized system could be used to cross-reference plant insect and disease problems with pesticides. The user would input the disease symptoms or insect description, and the computer would specify which chemicals to use. If a chemical was specified, one could find those diseases or insects against which it was effective and any notable characteristics or precautions that needed to be taken. A plant inventory system could provide the age or stage of growth for all plants, based upon their planting or transplanting date. Soon a computer may control a robot that transplants and separates diseased plants from healthy ones. Maybe it will even talk to them to make them grow better.

Glossary

It is very difficult to discuss computers without using some terms with special meanings. This glossary contains definitions for some words commonly used in the computer world. It is not a comprehensive list, and the definitions are not rigorous computer science ones, but they are intended to provide you with enough background to understand the rest of the book.

Address • programs and data are stored in an area of the computer known as its memory. The memory is divided into pieces called bytes, and each byte has its own unique address. It is similar to a post office. Each mail box in the post office has its own box number. To send a letter to a person, you must have the proper box number. To receive letters, you must open the box with the right number. The computer places information into its memory and takes information from its memory by using the memory addresses. The computer tells the memory which location it wishes to address, then reads what is there or writes something. The computer communicates with other devices like printers and the keyboard through devices called ports. Each port also has its own unique address, in the same manner as have memory locations. Memory and ports are addressable.

Acoustical coupler • a device for connecting a telephone handset to the computer. It is used to communicate with a computer via the telephone line.

ASCII • acronym for American Standard Code for Information Interchange. It refers to a standard developed for expressing letters, characters, and other symbols in a digital form that a computer can use. One could say that ASCII is to computers what Morse Code is to the telegraph.

Bug • a problem in a computer program or hardware. When a program does not perform its intended function, it has a bug in it. Similarly, if the computer hardware is malfunctioning, it has a bug in it.

Bus • an electronic path within a computer used to transmit electrical information from one point to another point. The information is "bussed" between points. Microcomputers have three buses: a data bus, an address bus, and a control bus.

The data bus is used to transmit data between the central processing unit and memory or other input/output devices, called ports. The address bus is used to tell the computer's memory which location will be used to either store or read a piece of information. All operations in a computer must be performed at the right time for the computer to function properly. The control bus controls this timing.

Central processing unit (CPU) • a module or component within a computer responsible for fetching, understanding, and executing instructions that tell the computer what to do. In small computers, this CPU is commonly called the microprocessor, from which we get the term *microcomputer*. A microcomputer is a computer that uses a microprocessor as its central processing unit.

Clock • a computer clock is a reference timing source that generates a series of accurately timed pulses. The computer uses these pulses as a timing reference for performing its various functions. Each act that the computer performs takes a set amount of time, which is measured in number of clock pulses. Different actions taken by the central processor require varying numbers of clock pulses. The upper limit to the clock speed is determined by the electrical characteristics of the computer's electronic components. Each component takes a finite amount of time to respond. Computers with higher speed clocks usually contain components with faster response times and often cost more. Typical clock speeds for microcomputers range from less than one million cycles per second (one MHz or one megahertz) to 12 MHz; many are no higher than 4 MHz. Clock speed is not linearly related to how many operations per second a computer can perform. If two otherwise identical computers have different speed clocks, the one with the faster clock will execute more quickly than the one with the slower clock.

Compiler • a program that examines a user's program and converts all of the program statements into a numerical code (set of numbers) that the computer can understand. When the user's program is actually run, no time is lost in converting the instructions into a "computer-understandable" form. A compiled program may execute faster than an interpreted program.

The disadvantage of using a compiled language is that the entire program must be recompiled each time a change is made in the program. This problem is avoided with an interpreted language. Programs take longer to write in a compiled language than in an interpreted one, but they execute faster. It is a tradeoff between programming time and execution time. Short programs and longer ones used only a few times should be written in an interpreted language. Programs that will be used many times and have many steps or calculations which the computer must perform rapidly should be compiled.

Computer • an electronic device controlled by a set of instructions. It consists of a central processing unit, memory, and input/output facilities. A computer is capable of making logical decisions. A logical decision is one based upon whether a condition or set of conditions is TRUE or FALSE. All communications within a computer are in the form of zeroes and ones, so everything is a zero or one, TRUE or FALSE.

Computer language • a set of commands and relationships which can be understood by a computer. Just as you speak English, French, Spanish, etc., a computer may speak BASIC, FORTRAN, or COBOL. Different computer languages have been designed for different purposes. Some are intended for business applications, some for graphics, some for scientific applications, and some for more specialized functions such as controlling robots.

Execute • to actually perform the instructions in a computer program. A computer runs or executes a program; the terms are synonymous.

File • a set of records. Data and computer programs are kept on cassette tapes or disks in files. These files are similar to a box containing recipes or a book of addresses. If the recipes or addresses were stored on a cassette or disk for the computer to use them, they would be stored in files.

Hardware • the physical components of the computer. Hardware includes the integrated circuits, monitor, keyboard, storage devices, printers, etc. If it is a part of a computing system that you can actually touch, it is hardware.

Hardware compatible • two devices are hardware compatible if they can be physically connected together. This does not necessary mean that they can actually function together or communicate with each other.

INPUT/OUTPUT • the transfer of information between the central processing unit and the "outside world." An I/O device could be a printer, track ball, light pen, keyboard, or pushbutton switch.

Integer number • a whole number with no decimal point. An integer can have either a positive or a negative value.

Interpreter • a computer program used to "interpret" commands written in a particular language into a form that the computer can understand and act upon. BASIC is often an interpreted language. When a BASIC program is run, the interpreter translates each statement into a form that the processor can understand. If a statement is executed 20 times, it is interpreted each time it is used. Interpreted languages are slower than compiled languages, but are easier to use. An interpreted language is easy to use because mistakes are easy to correct. Statements can be added or deleted from an interpreted program very easily. They cannot be with a compiled language.

Keyboard • a set of keys usually arranged in a layout similar to the keys on a typewriter and connected to the input section of a computer. Information and commands are often placed into the computer through the use of a keyboard.

Mass storage device • a device for storing data and programs. The typical ones used in microcomputer applications are cassette tapes, floppy diskettes, and sometimes hard disks. They enable the user to save programs and data and recall them for later use. A mass storage device allows a computer to work with more data and larger programs than it can hold in memory at one time. It allows the computer to examine only part of the data at a time or to divide a program into sections and only have one section in its memory at a time. It also allows the computer's random memory to be devoted to the task at hand.

The cassette tape • cassette storage is the cheapest form of data and program storage. Many small computers come with an audio cassette interface as standard equipment. To load a program into the computer from a cassette, you attach a tape player to the computer, turn on the player, and type a keyboard command to load the program. A few minutes later the program is loaded into the machine and ready to run. Programs are similarly saved on cassettes. Different microcomputers read from and write to cassettes at different speeds and with different methods. The magnetic cassette needs to be of a high quality. Cheap, low-grade cassettes increase the risk of losing stored information. Several programs can be stored on a single cassette.

There are some inherent limitations with cassette tapes. They are much slower to read from and write to than are floppy diskettes and hard disks. It may take ten to a hundred times as long to load a program from cassette as compared to loading from a diskette. Signal level is very important. If the volume control on the tape player is too low or too high, the computer can not read the program. Tone control is important on some players. Tape player head alignment is another important factor. I have tried as many as four different tape players before I could find one that would load some programs I had purchased. Many of the problems associated with reading and writing with cassettes can be eliminated if the same tape recorder is used for both recording and playback and if the read/write heads are kept clean.

Another limitation is due to the fact that a cassette is by nature a "sequential-access" device. That means if there are four programs on a tape, you can not read the fourth one until you either read the first three or advance the tape to where the fourth program begins.

If possible, use a tape player with a tape counter and advance to the desired area on the tape before reading it. The slow speed of cassettes makes working with data a problem, particularly if there are a large number of data points and you need to examine or change only a few of them. Use floppy disks or hard disks instead of cassettes if at all possible.

The floppy diskette • the diskette, sometimes called a floppy diskette or floppy disk, is a thin, flexible, nonmetallic disk covered with a metal oxide coating used to store and recall information. The information is recorded magnetically as a series of ones and zeroes, similar to a cassette tape. A diskette comes in a paper sleeve that should never be removed. The diskette and sleeve are placed in a disk drive that spins the diskette. As it spins, a read/write head moves back and forth just above the surface of the disk and transfers information to and from the surface by magnetizing the coating with a particular pattern or reading the pattern already there. When the diskette is removed, the information is retained on its surface. Information can be stored and recalled from a diskette several times faster than with a cassette. If a particular set of information (called a file) is needed, other files on the diskette do not have to be examined first, regardless of the order in which they were placed on the diskette.

Diskettes come in two common sizes: 5.25 inches and 8 inches in diameter. The larger the diskette, the more information it can hold. The term *density* is used to describe how densely the information is packed onto the diskette's surface. A double-density diskette can hold twice as much information as a single-density diskette of the same size used on the same machine. The capacity of a diskette is dependent upon the disk controlling device. Single-density, single-sided 5.25-inch diskettes commonly store from 90 kilobytes to 160 kilobytes of information. Double-sided diskettes have information stored on both sides. A double-density, double-sided diskette could contain four times as much information as a single-sided, single-density diskette. An 8-inch single-density, single-sided diskette will contain about 240 kilobytes of information. An 8-inch double-density, double-sided diskette can contain nearly one megabyte of information. Some new diskettes coming into the marketplace are 3 inches to 3.5 inches in diameter and have very large storage capacities compared to the conventional 5.25- and 8-inch diskettes.

Diskettes are very sensitive and can be damaged when handled improperly. The exposed surfaces of the diskette should never be touched. They should be kept away from high temperatures such as would develop in a parked car in the summer. Strong magnetic fields can also destroy the information recorded on a disk. Keep disks away from magnets and electric motors. Diskette drives are very expensive compared to cassette recorder/players. As with all other information storage devices, always have at least two copies of all important programs and data. Extra diskettes are very cheap compared to the cost of replacing lost data and programs.

The hard disk • the hard disk contains one or more rigid platters within a protective enclosure. Information is stored magnetically on hard disks somewhat like on flexible diskettes. The hard disk is placed in a hard disk drive. It spins at a very high speed (typically 3600 rpm), and data transfer is several times faster than for diskette drives. Storage capacity is also much larger and is usually rated in megabytes instead of kilobytes of storage. The cost for hard disks and their drives is also much higher, but the cost per unit of information storage capacity may actually be less than with other forms of mass storage. They are valuable when large amounts of information need to be accessed quickly, as in an inventory control system with several thousand parts. When treated carelessly, hard disks can be easily damaged. A particle smaller than a human hair can permanently damage one. Hard disk drives always use very fine air filters. Most of the ones used with microcomputer systems are completely sealed to prevent contaminants from damaging them.

When considering a hard disk in a system, make certain there is some kind of backup system. A backup system is some method for making a copy of everything on the disk. If something happens to the disk, there is another copy of the information that is still good. Never assume that you can get by without backing up both your data and your programs. The old rule that the probability of a system failure increases with the importance of the system seems to hold quite well with computers. The more convenient the backup system is to use, the more likely it will actually be used. If backup is with diskettes, many people are not willing to sit and place 50 or 70 diskettes into the system until all of the information is backed up. The backup method should require as little operator time as possible, and should be as simple as possible.

Memory • a set of electronic, addressable storage locations within the computer used to store programs and data. The memory is contained within one or more integrated circuits.

The smallest unit of addressable memory is the byte. A byte consists of eight binary digits, or bits. Each byte can have one of 256 values, since there are 256 possible unique combinations of 8 binary digits.

The memory capacity of personal computers is usually specified in kilobytes of RAM and abbreviated as "K." One kilobyte is equal to 1024 bytes. A 16K computer has 16 × 1024 bytes, or 16,384 bytes, of memory available for program and data storage. For most micro-computers, the maximum addressable memory in the form of both ROM and RAM is either 64K or 1024K (1024 kilobytes = one mega-byte), depending upon the microprocessor. A few microcomputers can address up to four megabytes of memory. There are two primary types of memory: RAM and ROM.

RAM (random-access memory) • memory locations within a computer that contain information which can be changed. The computer can read what is in RAM, and it can store information there. Random-access memory locations can be addressed in any order for reading or writing information. In one program a particular part of the RAM may have data in it, and in another program some part of the program itself may be stored in that same space. Whenever the machine is turned off, whatever is in RAM disappears and is lost to the user.

RAM is more flexible than ROM since the same space can be used for different things. It could contain a BASIC interpreter today and a word processing program tomorrow. The amount of RAM within a computer determines how much data and how large a program it can contain at any one moment. It may be a little misleading for RAM to be called random access while ROM is not. Both types can have any memory location accessed in any order. Perhaps it should be renamed read and write memory since the difference between it and ROM is that information cannot be written into ROM memory as it can in RAM.

ROM (read-only memory) • memory locations available only for reading by the computer. Information stored in ROM cannot be changed, and is not lost when the machine is turned off. ROM is used to store programs or data that are never changed and are needed whenever the system is used. It cannot be used by the computer to store information created while running a program. Many microcomputers have their BASIC language interpreter stored in ROM so that it is available whenever the machine is turned on.

Microprocessor • that part of a microcomputer that fetches program instructions and executes them. The microprocessor processes the program statements.

Modem • acronym for modulator/demodulator. A modem is a device used to send and receive information from a computer via a tele-phone line. It can be plugged directly into a telephone jack or used with a telephone handset and an acoustical coupler. Sometimes it is called a direct-connect modem.

Monitor • a video screen used by the computer to communicate results and other information to the user. A monitor is considered to be an output device by the computer.

Program • a computer program is a set of instructions that tells the computer what to do and how to do it. Computer programs are also referred to as SOFTWARE or CODE. A program must be in the computer's memory for the computer to use it.

Real number • a number containing a decimal point.

Reset • to stop whatever the computer is doing, destroy whatever is in its memory, and behave as if it had just been turned on.

Software • same as PROGRAM.

Software compatible • software is compatible with a particular computer if it will run correctly on that computer. Software compatibility is a major problem with different types of microcomputers. A program that will run on one kind of computer will quite often not run on another type.

Subroutine • a section of a computer program that performs one or more tasks. It is used in the program whenever that particular set of tasks needs to be performed. Subroutines are used whenever the tasks need to be performed many times during a computer program. They eliminate the need for rewriting a repeated part of the program every time it is needed. Whenever the program needs to use a subroutine, it "calls" it. After the subroutine is finished, the program continues whatever it was doing before the subroutine was called.

Suggested reading

AgriComp • 1001 East Walnut, Suite 201, Columbia MO 65201. "The Reference for Farm Computing." A bimonthly magazine devoted to the use of microcomputers in farming. A good source for VisiCalc® applications and for advertisers of agricultural software.

Agricultural Computing • Doane-Western, Inc., 8900 Manchester Road, St. Louis MO 63144. "A Doane-Western Newsletter for Computer Users in Agriculture." A monthly newsletter. Subscription includes binder with reference materials including several agricultural software suppliers and specifications for many microcomputers.

BYTE • BYTE Subscriptions, PO Box 590, Martinsville NJ 08836. "the small systems journal." A large (500–700 pages) monthly magazine written for those with interests in computer programming, hardware design and building, and computer controls, in addition to the user.

Compute! • PO Box 5406, Greensboro NC 27403. "The Journal For Progressive Computing." A monthly magazine devoted to computers based upon the 6502 microprocessor (includes PET™, Apple®, Atari®, OSI™, and others.)

Creative Computing • PO Box 13010, Philadelphia PA 19101. "The #1 magazine of computer applications and software." A monthly magazine for microcomputer users. Equipment and program reviews, columns devoted to several popular microcomputers. Aimed at both the user and the programmer.

Interface Age • PO Box 1234, Cerritos CA 90701. "Computing for Business and Home." A monthly magazine for users of small computers both at home and in business.

Personal Computing • 4 Disk Drive, PO Box 1423, Riverton NJ 08077. A monthly magazine written for the person who wants to use the computer without too much concern for the internal operations of the equipment. Good general purpose magazine.

The Portable Companion • Osborne Computer Corporation, 26538 Danti Court, Hayward CA 94545. "For Osborne™ Computer Users." A bimonthly publication for users of the Osborne™ portable computer.

80 Micro • Subscription Dept., PO Box 981, Farmingdale NY 11737. "The magazine for TRS-80™ users." Monthly magazine devoted primarily to Radio Shack® equipment and programs, and other equipment and programs compatible with Radio Shack®. Reviews and evaluations of hardware and programs.

---

*PET™ is a trademark of Commodore Business Machines. OSI™ is a trademark of Open Systems, Inc.

Index